LAURENCE GARDNER is an internationally known sovereign genealogist and historical lecturer. Distinguished as the Chevalier Labhràn de St Germain, he is Presidential Attaché to the European Council of Princes, a constitutional advisory body established in 1946. He is also Prior of the Sacred Kindred of St. Columba and a Fellow of the Society of Antiquaries of Scotland. Formally attached to the Noble Order of the Guard of St. Germain, founded by King James VII of Scots in 1692 and ratified by King Louis XIV of France, he is the appointed Jacobite Historiographer Royal.

BLOODLINE
◆ OF THE
HOLY GRAIL
THE HIDDEN LINEAGE OF JESUS REVEALED

LAURENCE GARDNER

THE CHEVALIER LABHRÀN DE SAINT GERMAIN

BARNES
&NOBLE
BOOKS
NEW YORK

© Element Books Ltd 2000

Text © Laurence Gardner 1996

This edition published by Barnes & Noble, Inc
by arrangement with Element Books Limited

2000 Barnes & Noble Books

M 10 9 8 7 6 5 4 3 2 1

ISBN 0-7607-2083-5

A CIP catalogue record for this book is available from the British Library

ELEMENT BOOKS LIMITED
Editorial Director: Sue Hook
Group Production Director: Clare Armstrong

Produced and packaged by The Book Laboratory, Inc., Mill Valley, CA
Designed by i4 Design, Sausalito, CA

Printed at Butler and Tanner Ltd, Frome and London

CONTENTS

Bible references are from
AUTHORIZED KING JAMES VERSION
Oxford Edition

LIST OF MAPS

LIST OF CHARTS

FOREWORD

Bloodline of the Holy Grail is a remarkable achievement in the field of genealogical research. Rare is the historian acquainted with such compelling facts as are gathered in this work. The revelations are entirely fascinating and will surely be appreciated by many as real treasures of enlightenment. Herein is the vital story of those fundamental issues which helped to shape the Christian Church in Europe and the Crusader States.

To some, aspects of this book will perhaps appear heretical in nature. It is the right of any individual to take this view since the inherent disclosures are somewhat removed from the orthodox tradition. However, the fact remains that Chevalier Labhràn has penetrated the very depths of available manuscripts and archival data concerning the subject, moving far beyond the bounds of any conventional domain. The resultant unveiled knowledge is presented in a very articulate, interesting and tantalizing manner.

This work offers an incredible insight into centuries of strategic governmental alignments, together with their associated deceits and intrigues. For around two thousand years, the destinies of millions of people have been manipulated by unique, though often whimsical, personalities, who have perverted the spiritual aspirations of our civilization. With marvelous detail, the author has removed the constraints of vested interest to relate numerous suppressed accounts of our heritage. In so doing, he resurrects the politically silenced history of a resolute royal dynasty which the Church has long sought to vanquish in order to further its own ends. Now, in this new age of understanding, may the truth prevail, and may the Phoenix rise once again.

HRH Prince Michael of Albany
Head of the Royal House of Stewart

ACKNOWLEDGEMENTS

For their valued assistance in the preparation of this work, I am indebted to the good offices of the Celtic Church of the Sacred Kindred of Saint Columba, the Royal House of Stewart, the European Council of Princes and the Order of Knights Templars of Jerusalem. I would similarly like to thank all the archivists and librarians who have aided my quest, especially those at The British Library, Bibliothèque Nationale de France, Bibliothèque de Bordeaux, Somerset County Library, Birmingham Central Library, Glasgow Mitchell Library and the National Library of Scotland.

Since this book is very much a synthesis of interrelated subject matter, I am greatly beholden to those specialist authors whose individual mastery in their respective fields has facilitated the coverage of specific aspects. Their personal research, expertise and pre-eminent published works have been invaluable. Apart from a comprehensive Bibliography, selected reading material is identified within the Notes and References and attention is drawn to certain writers in the general text.

My utmost gratitude is due to HRH Prince Michael of Albany for affording me privileged access to Household and Chivalric papers. I am also thankful to my wife, Angela, and son, James, for their forbearance during my time-consuming endeavor.

To those many friends who have smoothed the path of this venture in one way or another I offer my appreciation. In particular, I am grateful to John Baldock, Chev. David Roy Stewart, Chev. Jack Robertson, Rev. David Cuthbert Stalker, Karen Lyster, Gretchen Schroeder, Helen Wagner, Stephen Knight, Ron Saunders, Michael Deering, Chris Rosling, Philip Dunn, Julie Foakes and Dr. A. R. Kittermaster.

My thanks are due, of course, to Michael Mann, David Alexander, Penny Stopa and all my colleagues at Element Books in Britain and America.

For their generous support in aiding my work internationally, my special thanks to JZ Knight and all at Ramtha's School of Enlightenment, to Nancy Simms of Entropic Fine Art, to Christina Zohs of *The Golden Thread* and to Duncan Roads, Ruth Parnell and Marcus Allen of *Nexus*. Also to the directors of Multi MediaQuest International for their production of the *Bloodline* lecture recordings and for assisting with this special edition.

My thankful recognition is due to Sir Peter Robson for his artistic liaison and for the specially conceived painting, *Bloodline of the Holy Grail* <http://www.entropic-art.com/>. Similarly, to the composer, Sir Adrian Wagner who, in the family tradition of such masterworks as *Lohengrin* and *Parsifal*, has endorsed this book with his companion album, *Holy Spirit and the Holy Grail* <http://www.mediaquest.co.uk/awhshg.html>.

Finally, I must convey my gratitude to all those readers who have supported and encouraged my work since the publication of the first edition of *Bloodline*. Especially to those many thousands who have written to me with so many useful comments and contributions, which have helped to pave the way towards this colour Millennium Edition.

Laurence Gardner

On page 397 in Appendix IV of the 1996 first edition of *Bloodline of the Holy Grail*, a *Sinclair Genealogist* article concerning Christopher Columbus was inadvertently credited to its publisher, H. S. 'Pete' Cummings, Jnr, instead of to its author. With apologies, the credit in this regard should have been to Ian F. Brown.

Dedicated to the Memory

of

Dr. Whitman Pearson,

a questing pilgrim of the eternal Grail

Here is the Book of thy descent.

Here begins the Book of the Sangraél.

The Perlesvaus

Also by the same Author:
GENESIS OF THE GRAIL KINGS

Recommended in conjunction with this work:
THE FORGOTTEN MONARCHY OF SCOTLAND
by HRH Prince Michael of Albany

Frontispiece:
The red caped priestess Mary Magdalene in Provence.
Netherlandish, 16th century

I

ORIGINS OF THE BLOODLINE

Whom does the Grail Serve?

Following the Jewish Revolt in Jerusalem during the first century AD, the Roman overlords were reputed to have destroyed all records concerning the Davidic legacy of Jesus the Messiah's family. The destruction was far from complete, however, and relevant documents were retained by Jesus's heirs, who brought the Messianic heritage from the Near East to the West. As confirmed by the *Ecclesiastical History* of Eusebius, the fourth-century Bishop of Caesarea,[1] these heirs were called the Desposyni (ancient Greek for 'of the Master'),[2] a hallowed style reserved exclusively for those in the same family descent as Jesus.[3] Theirs was the sacred legacy of the Royal House of Judah - a dynastic bloodline that lives on today.

During the course of this book, we shall study the compelling story of this sovereign lineage by unfolding a detailed genealogical account of the Messianic Blood Royal (the *Sangréal*) in direct descent from Jesus and his brother James. However, in order to cover this ground, it will first be necessary to consider the Old and New Testament Bible stories from a different perspective to that normally conveyed. This will not be a rewriting of history, but a reshaping of familiar accounts bringing history back to its original base, rather than perpetuating the myths of strategic restyling by those with otherwise vested interests.

Throughout the centuries, an ongoing Church and governmental conspiracy has prevailed against the Messianic inheritance. This heightened when Imperial Rome diverted the course of Christianity to suit an alternative ideal and has continued to the present day.

Many apparently unconnected events of history have in fact been chapters of that same continuing suppression of the line. From the Jewish Wars of the first century through to the eighteenth-century American Revolution and beyond, the machinations have been perpetuated by English and European governments in collaboration with the Anglican and Roman Catholic Churches. In their attempts to constrain the royal birthright of Judah, the High Christian movements have installed various figurehead regimes, including Britain's own House of Hanover – Saxe-Coburg – Gotha. Such administrations have been compelled to uphold specific religious doctrines, while others have been deposed for preaching religious forbearance.

Now, at the turn of a new Millennium, this is a time for reflection and reform in the civilized world - and to accomplish such reform it is appropriate to consider the errors and successes of the past. For this purpose there is no better record than that which exists within the chronicles of the Sangréal.

The definition, *Holy Grail*, first appeared in the Middle Ages as a literary concept, based (as will be later discussed) on a series of scribal misinterpretations. It derived immediately as a translation from *Saint Grail* and from the earlier

The Roman Conquest of Jerusalem,
by Nicolas Poussin, 1594-1665

forms, *San Graal* and *Sangréal*. The Ancient Order of the Sangréal, a dynastic Order of the Scots Royal House of Stewart, was directly allied to the continental European Order of the Realm of Sion[4] and of the knights of both Orders were adherents of the Sangréal, which defines the true Blood Royal (the *Sang Réal*) of Judah: the *Bloodline of the Holy Grail*.

Quite apart from its dynastic physical aspect, the Holy Grail also has a spiritual dimension. It has been symbolized by many things, but as a material item it is most commonly perceived as a chalice, especially a chalice that contains, or once contained, the life-blood of Jesus. The Grail has additionally been portrayed as a vine, weaving its way through the annals of time. The fruit of the vine is the grape, and from the grape comes wine. In this respect, the symbolic elements of the chalice and the vine coincide, for wine has long been equated with the blood of Jesus. Indeed, this tradition sits at the very heart of the Eucharist (Communion), and the perpetual blood of the Grail chalice represents no less than the enduring Messianic bloodline.

In esoteric Grail lore, the chalice and vine support the ideal of 'service', whereas the blood and wine correspond to the eternal spirit of 'fulfilment'. The spiritual Quest of the Grail is, therefore, a desire for fulfillment through giving and receiving service. That which is called the Grail Code is itself a parable for the human condition, in that it is the quest of us all to achieve through service. The problem is that the precept of the Code has been overwhelmed by an avaricious society complex, based on the notion of the 'survival of the fittest'. Today, it is plain that wealth, rather than health, is a major stepping-stone towards being socially fit, whilst another criterion is obedience to the law.

Above such considerations, however, there is a further requirement: the requirement to toe the party line while paying homage to the demigods of power. This prerequisite has nothing to do with obeying the law or with behaving properly - it relies totally on not rocking the boat and on withholding opinions that do not conform. Those who break ranks are declared heretics, meddlers and troublemakers, and as such are deemed socially unfit by their governing establishment. Perceived social fitness is consequently attained by submitting to indoctrination and forsaking personal individuality in order to preserve the administrative *status quo*. By any standard of reckoning, this can hardly be described as a democratic way of life.

The democratic ideal is expressed as 'government *by* the people *for* the people'. To facilitate the process, democracies are organized on an electoral basis whereby the few represent the many. The representatives are chosen *by* the people to govern *for* the people - but the paradoxical result is generally their government *of* the people. This is contrary to all the principles of democratic community and has nothing whatever to do with *service*. It is, therefore, in direct opposition to the Grail Code.

At a national and local level, elected representatives have long managed to reverse the harmonious ideal by setting themselves upon pedestals above their electorate. By virtue of this, individual rights, liberties and welfare are controlled by political dictate, and such dictates determine who is socially fit and who is socially unfit at any given time. In many cases this even corresponds to decisions on who shall survive and who shall not. To this end, there are many who seek positions of influence for the sheer sake of gaining power over others. Serving their own interests, they become manipulators of society, causing the disempowerment of the majority. The result is that, instead of being rightly served, that same majority is reduced to a state of servitude.

Accordingly, *Bloodline of the Holy Grail* is not restricted in content to genealogies and tales of political intrigue, but its pages hold the key to the essential Grail Code - the key not only to a historical mystery but to a way of life. It is a book about good government and bad government. It tells how the patriarchal kingship of people was supplanted by dogmatic tyranny and the dictatorial overlordship of land. It is a journey of discovery through past ages, with its eye set firmly upon the future.

Whom does the Grail serve? It serves those who quest despite the odds - for they are the champions of enlightenment.

THE PAGAN IDOLS OF CHRISTENDOM

In the course of our journey we shall confront a number of assertions which may at first seem startling, but this is often the case when setting historical matters to rights, for most of us have been conditioned to accept certain interpretations of history as matters of fact. To a large extent we have all learned history by way of strategic propaganda, whether Church or politically motivated. It is all part of the control process; it separates the masters from the servants and the fit from the unfit. Political history has, of course, long been written by its masters - the few who decide the fate and fortunes of the many. Religious history is no different, for it is designed to implement control through fear of the unknown. In this way the religious masters have retained their supremacy at the expense of devotees who genuinely seek enlightenment and salvation.

In biblical terms our Grail quest begins with the Creation, as defined in the book of Genesis. A little more than two centuries ago, in 1779, a consortium of London booksellers issued the mammoth 42-

volume *Universal History*, a work that came to be much revered and which stated with considered assurance that God's work of Creation began on 21 August 4004 BC.[5] A debate ensued over the precise month, for some theologians reckoned that 21 March was the more likely date. All agreed, however, that the year was accurate and everyone accepted that there were only six days between cosmic nothingness and the emergence of Adam.

At the time of publication, Britain was in the grip of the Industrial Revolution. It was an unsettled period of extraordinary change and development but, as with today's rapid rate of advancement, there were social prices to pay. The prized skills and crafts of yesteryear became obsolete in the face of mass production and society was regrouped to accommodate an economically based community structure. A new breed of 'winners' emerged, while the majority floundered in an unfamiliar environment that bore no relation to the customs and standards of their upbringing. Rightly or wrongly, this phenomenon is called 'progress' and the relentless criterion of progress is that very precept propounded by the English naturalist Charles Darwin: the 'survival of the fittest'.[6] The problem is that people's chances of survival are often diminished because they are ignored or exploited by their masters - those same pioneers who forge the route to progress, aiding (if not guaranteeing) their own survival.

It is easy now to appreciate that the 1779 *Universal History* was wrong. We know that the world was not created in 4004 BC. We also know that Adam was not the first man on Earth.[7] Such archaic notions have been outgrown - but to the people of the late eighteenth century this impressive *History* was the product of men more learned than most and it was, naturally, presumed correct. It is therefore worth posing ourselves a question at this stage: How many of today's accepted facts of science and history will also be outgrown in the light of future discoveries?

Dogma is not necessarily truth; it is simply a fervently promoted interpretation of truth based on available facts. When new influential facts are presented, scientific dogma changes as a matter of course - but this is rarely the case with religious dogma. In this book we are particularly concerned with the attitudes and teachings of a Christian Church which pays no heed to discoveries and revelations, and which still upholds much of the incongruous dogma that dates from medieval times. As H. G. Wells so astutely observed during the early 1900s, the religious life of Western nations is 'going on in a house of history built upon sand'.

Traditional concept of the Creation.
19th-century engraving
from a painting by N. Blakey

**Imperial Britannia receives
the Riches of the East**

Charles Darwin's theory of evolution in *The Descent of Man* in 1871[8] caused no personal harm to Adam, but any thought of his being the first living human was naturally discredited. Like all the organic life forms on the planet, humans had evolved by genetic mutation and natural selection through hundreds of thousands of years. The announcement of this fact struck religious minded society with horror. Some simply refused to accept the new doctrine, but many fell into despair. If Adam and Eve were not the primal parents, there was no Original Sin and the very reason for atonement was, therefore, without foundation!

The majority completely misunderstood the concept of Natural Selection. They deduced that if survival was restricted to the fittest then success must be dependent on outdoing one's neighbour! Thus, a new skeptical and ruthless generation was born. Egotistical nationalism flourished as never before and domestic deities were venerated as were the pagan gods of old. Symbols of national identity - such as Britannia and Hibernia - became the new idols of Christendom.

From this unhealthy base was generated an imperialist disease and the stronger, advanced countries claimed the right to exploit less developed nations. The new age of empire building began with an undignified scramble for territorial domain. The German Reich was founded in 1871 through the amalgamation of hitherto separate states. Other states combined to form the Austro-Hungarian Empire. The Russian Empire expanded considerably and, by the 1890s, the British Empire occupied no less than one-fifth of the entire global land mass. This was the impassioned era of resolute Christian missionaries, many of them dispatched from Queen Victoria's Britain. With the religious fabric sorely rent at home, the Church sought a revised justification abroad. The missionaries were especially busy in such places as India and Africa, where the people already had their own beliefs and had never heard of Adam. More importantly, though, they had never heard of Charles Darwin!

In Britain, a new intermediate stratum in society had emerged from the employers of the

Assassination of Archduke Francis Ferdinand
at Sarajevo on 28 June 1914

Industrial Revolution. This burgeoning middle class set the true aristocracy and the governing establishment far beyond the reach of people at large, effectively creating a positive class structure - a system of divisions in which everyone had a designated place. The chieftains wallowed in Arcadian pursuits, while the merchant opportunists competed for station through conspicuous consumption. The workingman accepted his serfdom with songs of allegiance, a dream of Hope and Glory, and a portrait of the tribal priestess Britannia above his mantelshelf.

Students of history knew it would not be long before empires set their sights against each other, and they forecast a day when competing powers would meet in mighty opposition. The conflict began when France endeavored to recover Alsace-Lorraine from German occupation, while the pair battled over the territory's iron and coal reserves. Russia and Austria-Hungary locked horns in a struggle for dominion of the Balkans and there were disputes resulting from colonial ambitions in Africa and elsewhere. The fuse was lit in June 1914 when a Serbian nationalist murdered Archduke Francis Ferdinand, the heir to the Austrian throne. At this, Europe exploded into a great war, largely instigated by Germany. Hostilities were commenced against Serbia, Russia, France and Belgium, and the counter-offensive was led by Britain. The struggle lasted for more than four years, coming to an end when a revolt erupted in Germany and Emperor (Kaiser) William II fled the country.

Following all the technological advancements of a manufacturing age, history had made little progress in social terms. Engineering achievements had led to unprecedented martial ability, while Christianity had become so fragmented as to be barely recognizable. Britain's pride emerged intact, but the German Reich was not of a mind to take its losses lightly. With the old regime overthrown, a fervent new party rose to dominance. Its despotic Fuehrer (leader), Adolf Hitler, annexed Austria in 1937 and swept into Poland two years later. The second great war - truly a World War - had begun: the fiercest territorial struggle to date. It was waged through six years and was centered upon the very core beliefs of religion itself: the rights of everyone in a civilized environment.

Quite suddenly, the Church and the people realized that religion was not, and never had been, about patriarchs and miracles. It was about belief in a neighbourly way of life, an application of moral standards and ethical values, of faith and charity, along with the constant quest for freedom and deliverance. At last any continuing general dispute about the evolutionary nature of human descent was put aside; that was the province of scientists and the majority relaxed in acceptance of the fact.

The Church emerged as a far less fearful opponent of scholars, and the new environment was more agreeable to all concerned. For many, the text of the Bible had no longer to be regarded as inviolable dogma and venerated for its own sake. Religion was embodied in its precepts and principles, not in the paper on which it was printed.

This new perspective gave rise to endless speculative possibilities. If Eve had truly been the only woman in existence and her only offspring were three sons, then with whom did her son Seth unite to father the tribes of Israel? If Adam was not the first man on Earth, what actually was his significance? Who or what were the angels? The New Testament also had its share of mysteries. Who were the apostles? Did the miracles really happen?

And most importantly, did the Virgin Birth and the Resurrection genuinely take place as described?

We shall consider all of these questions before we embark on the trail of the Grail Bloodline itself. In fact, it is imperative to understand Jesus's historical and environmental background in order to comprehend the facts of his marriage and parental fatherhood. As we progress, many readers will find themselves treading wholly new ground - but it is simply the ground that existed before it was carpeted and concealed by those whose motives were to suppress the truth for the sake of retaining control. Only by rolling back the carpet of strategic concealment can we succeed in our Quest for the Holy Grail.

BLOODLINE OF THE KINGS

It is now generally acknowledged that the opening chapters of the Old Testament do not represent the early history of the world as they appear to suggest.[9] More precisely, they tell the story of a family: a family that became a race comprising various tribes - a race that in turn became the Hebrew nation. If Adam was the first of a type, then he was apparently a progenitor of the Hebrews and the tribes of Israel.[10] Indeed, as described in this book's companion volume, *Genesis of the Grail Kings*, he was actually the first of a predestined line of priestly governors.

Two of the most intriguing Old Testament characters are Joseph and Moses. Each played an important role in the formation of the Hebrew nation and both have historical identities that can be examined quite independently of the Bible.

Genesis 41:39-43 tells how Joseph was made Governor of Egypt:

> And Pharaoh said unto Joseph ... Thou shalt be over my house and according unto thy word shall all my people be ruled: only in the throne will I be greater than thou ... and he made him ruler over all the land of Egypt.

Referring to Moses, Exodus 11:3 informs us similarly that:

> Moses was very great in the land of Egypt, in the sight of the Pharaoh's servants, and in the sight of the people.

Yet for all this status and prominence, neither Joseph nor Moses appear in any Egyptian record under their given biblical names.

The annals of Ramesses II (*c.*1304-1237 BC) specify that Semitic people were settled in the land of Goshen and it is further explained that they went there from Canaan for want of food. But why should Ramesses' scribes mention this Nile delta settlement at Goshen? According to standard Bible chronology, the Hebrews went to Egypt some three centuries before the time of Ramesses and made their exodus in about 1491 BC, long before he came to the throne. So, by virtue of this first-hand scribal record, the standard Bible chronology as generally promoted is seen to be incorrect.

Moses negotiates the Israelites'
freedom with the Pharaoh of Egypt,
by Gustave Doré, 1832-83

Statue of Pharaoh Ramesses II
(c.1304-1237 BC) at Luxor, Egypt

It is traditionally presumed that Joseph was sold into slavery in Egypt in the 1720s BC and was made Governor by the Pharaoh a decade or so later. Afterwards, his father Jacob (whose name was changed to Israel)[11] and seventy family members followed him into Goshen to escape the famine in Canaan. Notwithstanding this, Genesis 47:11, Exodus 1:11 and Numbers 33:30 all refer to 'the land of Ramesses' (Egyptian: 'the house of Ramesses')[12] - but this was a complex of grain storehouses built by the Israelites for Ramesses II in Goshen some 300 years after they were supposedly there!

It transpires, therefore, that the alternative Jewish Reckoning is more accurate than the Standard Chronology: Joseph was in Egypt not in the early eighteenth century BAD, but in the early fifteenth century BAD. There he was appointed Chief Minister to Tuthmosis IV (c.1413-1405 BAD). To the Egyptians, however, Joseph (Yusuf the Vizier) was known as Yuya and his story is particularly revealing - not just in relation to the biblical account of Joseph, but also in respect of Moses. The Cairo-born historian and linguist Ahmed Osman has made an in-depth study of these personalities in their contemporary Egyptian environment and his findings are of great significance.[13]

When Pharaoh Tuthmosis died, his son married his sibling sister Sitamun (as was the pharaonic tradition) so that he could inherit the throne as Pharaoh Amenhotep III. Shortly afterwards he also married Tiye, daughter of the Chief Minister (Joseph/Yuya). It was decreed, however, that no son born to Tiye could inherit the throne and, because of the overall length of her father Joseph's governorship, there was a general fear that the Israelites were gaining too much power in Egypt. So when Tiye became pregnant, the edict was given that her child should be killed at birth if a son. Tiye's Israelite relatives lived at Goshen and she owned a summer palace a little upstream at

Pharaoh Amenhotep III (c.1405-1367 BC) and the Egyptian crocodile god Sobek, the great Messeh

Zarw, where she went to have her baby. She did indeed bear a son, but the royal midwives conspired with Tiye to float the child downstream in a reed basket to the house of her father's half-brother Levi.

The boy, Aminadab (born c.1394 BAD), was duly educated in the eastern delta country by the Egyptian priests of Ra. Then, in his teenage years he went to live at Thebes. By that time, his mother had acquired more influence than the senior queen, Sitamun, who had never borne a son and heir to the Pharaoh, only a daughter who was called Nefertiti. In Thebes, Aminadab could not accept the Egyptian deities with their myriad idols and so he introduced the notion of Aten, an omnipotent God who had no image. Aten was thus an equivalent of the Hebrews' Adon - a title borrowed from the Phoenician and meaning 'Lord' - in line with Israelite teachings. At that time Aminadab (the Hebrew equivalent of Amenhotep: 'Amun is pleased') changed his name to Akhenaten (Servant of Aten).

Pharaoh Amenhotep then suffered a period of ill health and, since there was no direct male heir to the royal house, Akhenaten married his half-sister Nefertiti in order to rule as co-regent during this difficult time. In due course, however, when Amenhotep III died, Akhenaten was able to succeed as Pharaoh, gaining the official style of Amenhotep IV. He and Nefertiti had six daughters and a son called Tutankhaten.

The Pharaoh's daughter finding the baby Moses,
by Paolo Veronese, c.1575

Pharaoh Akhenaten closed all the temples of the Egyptian gods and built new temples to Aten. He also ran a household that was distinctly domestic - quite different from the kingly norm in ancient Egypt. On many fronts he became unpopular, particularly with the priests of the former national deity Amun (or Amen) and of the sun god Ra (or Re), as a result of which, plots against his life proliferated. Loud were the threats of armed insurrection if he did not allow the traditional gods to be worshipped alongside the faceless Aten. But Akhenaten refused

and was eventually forced to abdicate in short-term favor of his cousin Smenkhkare, who was succeeded by Akhenaten's son Tutankhaten. But, on taking the throne at the age of about eleven, Tutankhaten was obliged to change his name to Tutankhamen. He, in turn, was only to live and reign for a further nine or ten years, meeting his death while still comparatively young.

Akhenaten, meanwhile, was banished from Egypt. He fled with some retainers to the remote safety of Sinai, taking with him his royal sceptre topped with a brass serpent. To his supporters he remained very much the rightful monarch - the heir to the throne from which he had been ousted - and he was still regarded by them as the *Mose*, *Meses* or *Mosis*, meaning 'heir' or 'born of' - as in Tuthmosis ('born of Tuth') and Ramesses ('fashioned of Ra').

Evidence from Egypt indicates that Moses (Akhenaten) led his people from Pi-Ramesses (near modern Kantra) southwards, through Sinai, towards Lake Timash.[14] This was extremely marshy territory and, although it was manageable on foot with some difficulty, any pursuing horses and chariots would have foundered disastrously.

Pharaoh Akhenaten, the Mose of Egypt
(Amenhotep IV), c.1367 - 1361 BC

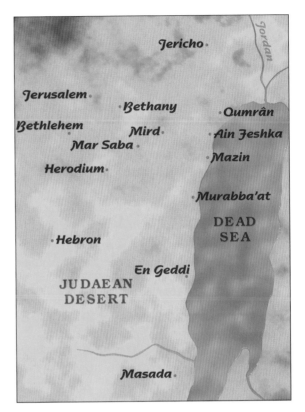

Qumrân - Land of the Scrolls

Among the retainers who fled with Moses were the families of Jacob (Israel): the Israelites. Then, at the instigation of their leader, they constructed the Tabernacle[15] and the Ark of the Covenant at the foot of Mount Sinai. Once Moses had died, they began their invasion of the country left by their forefathers so long before, but Canaan (Palestine) had changed considerably in the meantime, having been infiltrated by waves of Philistines and Phoenicians. The records tell of great sea battles and of massive armies marching to war. At length, the Israelites (under their new leader, Joshua) were successful and, once across the Jordan, they took Jericho from the Canaanites, gaining a real foothold in their traditional Promised Land.

Following Joshua's death, the ensuing period of rule by appointed Judges was a catalogue of disaster until the disparate Hebrew and Israelite tribes united under Saul, their first king, in about 1048 BC. Eventually, however, with the conquest of Canaan as complete as possible, David of Bethlehem married Saul's daughter to become King of Judah (corresponding to half the Palestinian territory) in around 1008 BC. Subsequently, he also acquired Israel (the balance of the territory) to become overall King of the Jews - and the reigning Bloodline of the Holy Grail had begun.

IN THE BEGINNING

JEHOVAH AND THE GODDESS

Together with the military exploits of the Israelites, the Old Testament describes the evolution of the Jewish faith from the time of Abraham. The story is not that of a unified nation devoted to the God Jehovah, but tells of a tenacious sect who fought against all odds to contrive the dominant religion of Israel. In their opinion, Jehovah was male, but this was a sectarian concept that gave rise to severe and manifold problems.

On the wider contemporary stage, it was generally understood that the creation of life must emanate from both male and female sources. Other religions - whether in Egypt, Mesopotamia or elsewhere - accordingly had deities of both sexes. The primary male god was generally associated with the sun or the sky, while the primary goddess had her roots in the earth, the sea and fertility. The sun gave its force to the earth and waters, from which sprang life: a very natural and logical interpretation.

In relation to such theistic ideas, one of the more flexible characters mentioned in biblical texts is King David's son, Solomon, celebrated not just for the magnificence and splendour of his reign, but for the wisdom of the man himself. Much later, Solomon's legacy was crucial to emergent Grail lore because he was the true advocate of religious toleration. Solomon was king centuries before the period of the Israelites' captivity in Babylon and he was very much a part of the old environment.

During Solomon's era, Jehovah was afforded considerable importance, but other gods were acknowledged as well. It was a spiritually uncertain age in which it was not uncommon for individuals to hedge their bets in respect of alternative deities. After all, with such a plethora of different gods and goddesses receiving homage in the region, it might have been shortsighted to decry all but one - for who was to say that the devout Hebrews had got it right!

In this regard, Solomon's renowned wisdom was based on considered judgment. Even though he worshipped Jehovah (the God of a minority sect) he had no reason to deny his subjects their

A presentation to King Solomon of Israel,
by Denise Bourbonnais

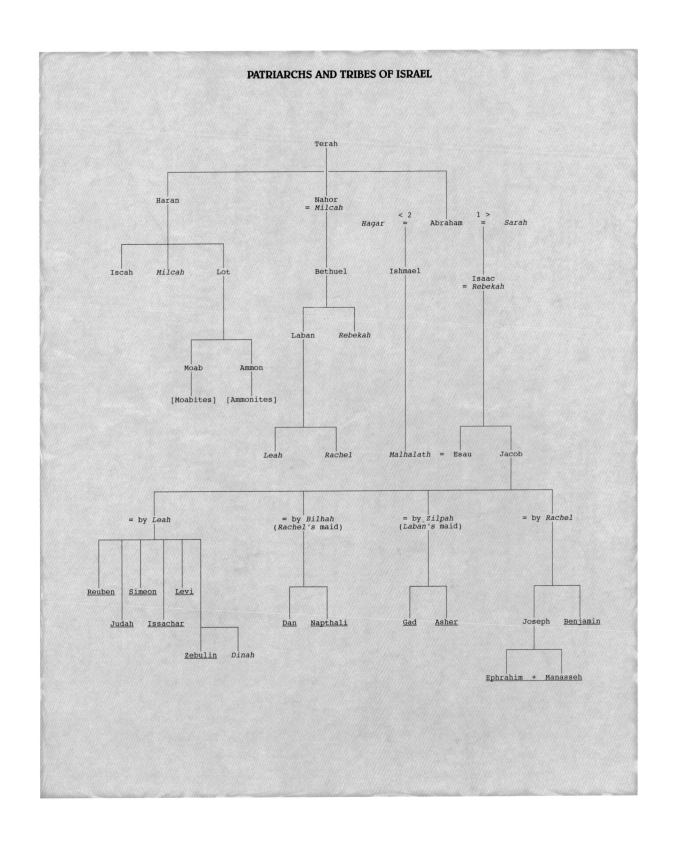

PATRIARCHS AND TRIBES OF ISRAEL

own gods (1 Kings 11:4-10). He even retained his own beliefs in the divine forces of nature, no matter who or what was at the head of them.

Veneration of the primary female deity was of long standing in Canaan, where she took the form of the goddess Ashtoreth. She was equivalent to Ishtar, the major goddess of the Babylonians. As Inanna, her Sumerian temple was at Uruk (the biblical Erech, modern Warka) in southern Mesopotamia, while in nearby Syria and Phoenicia she was reported by the ancient Greeks to have been called Astarte.

The Holy of Holies, or Inner Sanctum of Solomon's Temple, was deemed to represent the womb of Ashtoreth (alternatively called Asherah, as mentioned several times in the Old Testament). Ashtoreth was openly worshipped by the Israelites until the sixth century BC. As the Lady Asherah, she was the supernal wife of El, the supreme male

King Solomon,
by Simeon Solomon, c.1854

deity, and they were together the Divine Couple. Their daughter was Anath, Queen of the Heavens, and their son, the King of the Heavens, was called He. As time progressed, the separate characters of El and He were merged to become Jehovah. Asherah and Anath were then similarly conjoined to become Jehovah's female consort, known as the Shekinah or Matronit.

The name Jehovah is a late and somewhat Anglicized transliteration of Yahweh, which is itself a form of the four-consonantal Hebrew stem YHWH into which two vowels have been rightly or wrongly interpolated.[1] Originally, these four consonants (which later became a sort of acronym for the One God) represented the four members of the Heavenly Family: Y represented El the *Father*; H was Asherah the *Mother*; W corresponded to He the *Son*, and H was the *Daughter*, Anath. In accordance with the royal traditions of the time and region, God's mysterious bride, the Shekinah, was also reckoned to be his sister. In the Jewish cult of the Kabbalah (an esoteric discipline that reached its height in medieval times) God's dual male-female image was perpetuated. Meanwhile other sects perceived the Shekinah (or Matronit) as the female presence of God on Earth. The divine marital chamber was the Sanctuary of the Jerusalem Temple but, from the moment the Temple was destroyed, the Shekinah was destined to roam the Earth while the male aspect of Jehovah was left to rule the heavens alone.

In practical terms, the cementing of the Hebrew ideal of the one male God did not actually occur until after their fifty years of captivity in Babylon (*c*.586-536 BC). When the Israelites were first deported there by Nebuchadnezzar, they were effectively disparate tribes belonging to at least two major ethnic streams (Israel and Judah), but they returned to the Holy Land with a common national purpose as Jehovah's 'chosen people'.

Much of what we now know as the Old Testament (the Hebrew Bible) was first written down in Babylon.[2] It is hardly surprising, therefore, that Sumerian and Mesopotamian stories were grafted onto the early Jewish cultural tradition - including accounts of the Garden of Eden (the Paradise of Eridu[3]), the Flood[4] and the Tower of Babel.[5] The patriarch Abraham had migrated to Canaan from Ur of the Chaldees (in Mesopotamia), so the cultural grafting was justifiable, but the fact remains that stories such as that of Adam and Eve were by no means restricted to Hebrew tradition. In this regard, their lives and historical relevance are discussed at length in *Genesis of the Grail Kings*.

Alternatives to the Bible's version of the Adam and Eve story may be found in the writings of Greeks, Syrians, Egyptians, Sumerians and Abyssinians (ancient Ethiopians). Some accounts tell of Adam's first consort, Lilith, before he was enchanted by Eve. Lilith was handmaiden to the Shekinah and she left Adam because he tried to dominate her. Escaping to the Red Sea, she cried 'Why should I lie beneath you? I am your equal!' A Sumerian terracotta relief depicting Lilith (dating from around 2000 BC), shows her naked and winged, standing on the backs of two lions and holding the rods and rings of divine rulership and wisdom. Although not a goddess in the traditional

Israelites in chains before Nebuchadnezzar of Babylon.

13th century manuscript illustration

**Sumerian terracotta relief of Lilith,
with the rods and rings
of divine justice, c.2000 BC**

although the Jews were understood to be God's chosen people, Jehovah had not actually treated them very kindly. He was their all-powerful tribal Lord and had promised the patriarch Abraham to exalt their race above all others. And yet, for all that, they had faced only wars, famines, deportation and captivity! To counter the nation's growing disenchantment, the Books of the Prophets reinforced Jehovah's promise by announcing the Coming of a Messiah, an anointed King or Priest who would serve the people by leading them to salvation.[10]

This prophecy was sufficient to ensure the rebuilding of Solomon's Temple and the Wall of Jerusalem, but no Messianic savior appeared. The Old Testament ends at this point in the fourth century BC. Meanwhile, the bloodline of David continued, although not actively reigning. Then, more than 300 years later, a whole new chapter of sovereign history began when the revolutionary heir of Judah stepped boldly into the public domain. He was Jesus the Nazarene, the King *de jure* of Jerusalem.

SCROLLS AND TRACTATES

The Dead Sea Scrolls are now the most useful aids to understanding the Judaean culture of the pre-Gospel era,[11] but they were discovered by pure chance as recently as 1947. A Bedouin shepherd boy, Mohammed ed-Di'b, was searching for a lost goat in the cliff-hill caves of Qumrân, near Jericho, when he found a number of tall earthenware jars. Professional archaeologists were called in and excavations were subsequently undertaken - not only at Qumrân but at nearby Murabba'at and Mird in the

sense, her incarnate spirit was said to flourish in Solomon's most renowned lover, the Queen of Sheba. Lilith is described in the sacred book of the esoteric Mandaeans of Iraq as the Daughter of the Underworld[6] and, throughout history to the present day, she has represented the fundamental ethic of female opportunity.

When the Israelites returned from Babylon to Jerusalem, the first five Books of Moses[7] were collated into the Jewish *Torah* (the Law). The rest of the Old Testament was, however, kept separate. For a number of centuries, it was regarded with varying degrees of veneration and suspicion but, in time, the Books of the Prophets[8] became especially significant in stabilizing the Jewish heritage.[9] The main reason for hesitation was that,

THE HOUSE OF HEROD

37 BC - AD 99

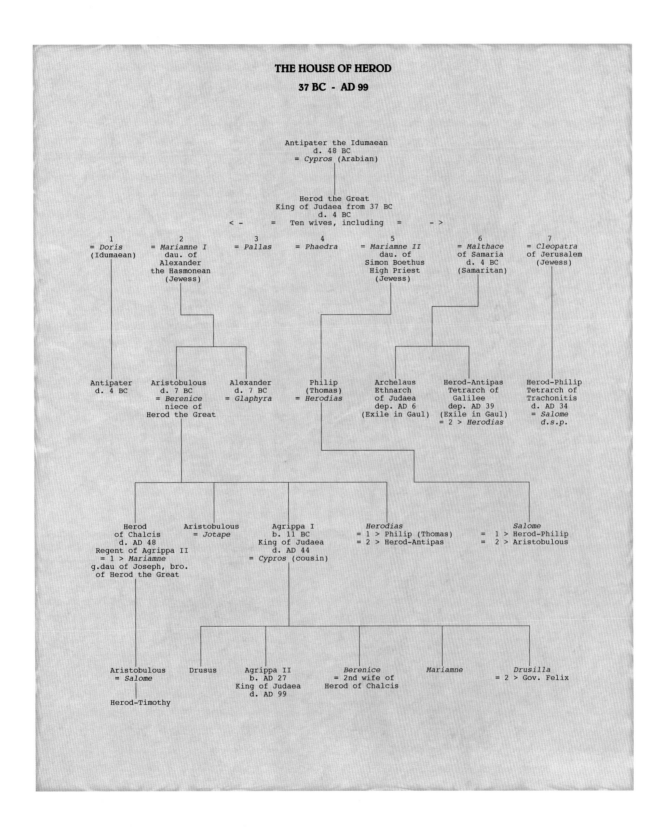

```
                          Antipater the Idumaean
                                 d. 48 BC
                            = Cypros (Arabian)


                             Herod the Great
                          King of Judaea from 37 BC
                                 d. 4 BC
                     < -   =  Ten wives, including  =    - >


     1              2            3          4            5              6              7
  = Doris     = Mariamne I    = Pallas   = Phaedra  = Mariamne II   = Malthace    = Cleopatra
 (Idumaean)     dau. of                               dau. of       of Samaria   of Jerusalem
              Alexander                             Simon Boethus     d. 4 BC      (Jewess)
             the Hasmonean                           High Priest    (Samaritan)
               (Jewess)                               (Jewess)


  Antipater   Aristobulous   Alexander   Philip      Archelaus     Herod-Antipas   Herod-Philip
  d. 4 BC     d. 7 BC        d. 7 BC     (Thomas)    Ethnarch      Tetrarch of     Tetrarch of
              = Berenice     = Glaphyra  = Herodias  of Judaea     Galilee         Trachonitis
              niece of                               dep. AD 6     dep. AD 39      d. AD 34
              Herod the Great                        (Exile in Gaul) (Exile in Gaul) = Salome
                                                                   = 2 > Herodias   d.s.p.


       Herod             Aristobulous   Agrippa I        Herodias              Salome
       of Chalcis        = Jotape       b. 11 BC         = 1 > Philip (Thomas) = 1 > Herod-Philip
       d. AD 48                         King of Judaea   = 2 > Herod-Antipas   = 2 > Aristobulous
       Regent of Agrippa II             d. AD 44
       = 1 > Mariamne                   = Cypros (cousin)
       g.dau of Joseph, bro.
       of Herod the Great


   Aristobulous   Drusus    Agrippa II      Berenice        Mariamne     Drusilla
   = Salome                 b. AD 27        = 2nd wife of                 = 2 > Gov. Felix
                            King of Judaea  Herod of Chalcis
   Herod-Timothy            d. AD 99
```

Wilderness of Judaea.[12] Many more jars were discovered in eleven different caves. Altogether the jars contained around 500 Hebrew and Aramaic manuscripts - among them Old Testament writings and numerous documents of community record, with some of their traditions dating back to about 250 BC. The Scrolls had been hidden during the Jewish Revolt against the Romans (between AD 66 and 70) and were never retrieved. The Old Testament book of Jeremiah (32:14) states prophetically, 'Thus saith the Lord of Hosts ... Take these evidences ... and put them in an earthen vessel, that they may continue many days'.[13]

Among the more important manuscript texts, the *Copper Scroll* lists an inventory and gives the locations for the treasures of Jerusalem and the Kedron Valley cemetery. The *War Scroll* contains a full account of military tactics and strategy. The *Manual of Discipline* details law and legal practice along with customary ritual and describes the

importance of a designated Council of Twelve to preserve the faith of the land. The fascinating *Habakkuk Pesher* gives a commentary on the contemporary personalities and important developments of the era. Also in the collection is a complete draft of Isaiah which, at more than 30 feet (around 9 metres) in length, is the longest scroll and is centuries older than any other known copy of that Old Testament book.

To complement these discoveries, another significant find relating to the post-Gospel era had been made in Egypt two years earlier. In December 1945 two peasant brothers, Mohammed and Khalifah Ali, were digging for fertilizer in a cemetery near the town of Nag Hammadi when they came upon a large sealed jar containing thirteen leather-bound books. The books' papyrus leaves contained an assortment of scriptures, written in the tradition that was later to be called Gnostic (esoteric insight). Inherently Christian works, but with Jewish overtones, they have become known as the *Nag Hammadi Library*.[14]

The books were written in the ancient Coptic language of Egypt during early Christian times. The Coptic Museum in Cairo ascertained that they were, in fact, copies of much older works originally composed in Greek. Indeed, some of the texts were discovered to have very early origins, incorporating traditions from before AD 50. Included in the fifty-two separate tractates are various religious texts and certain hitherto unknown Gospels, which tend to portray an environment very different from that described in the Bible. The cities of Sodom and Gomorrah, for example, are not presented as centres of wickedness and debauchery, but as cities of great wisdom and learning. More to our purpose, they describe a world in which Jesus gives his own account of the Crucifixion, and in which his relationship with Mary Magdalene reaches enlightening new proportions.

**Cliffhill cave at Qumrân,
land of the Scrolls**

Secret Codes of the New Testament

The excavations at Qumrân have produced relics dating from about 3500 BC, at which time (during the Bronze Age) the settlement was a Bedouin[15] camp. The period of formal occupation seems to have commenced in about 130 BC. Jewish chronicles describe a violent Judaean earthquake in 31 BC[16] and this is confirmed at Qumrân by a break between two distinct times of habitation.[17] According to the *Copper Scroll*, old Qumrân was called Sekhakha.

The second residential period began during the reign of Herod the Great (*c.*37-4 BC). Herod was an Idumaean Arab, installed as King of Judaea by the Roman authorities who had first taken control of the region under Julius Caesar. Apart from the evidence of the Scrolls, a collection of coins has also been amassed from the Qumrân settlement,[18] relating to a time-span from the Hasmonaean ruler John Hyrcanus (135-104 BC) to the Jewish Revolt of AD 66-70.

The uprising in 168 BC, in which the priestly caste of Hasmonaean Maccabees came to prominence, was prompted largely by the action of King Antiochus IV Epiphanes of Syria, who had foisted a system of Greek worship upon the Jewish community. The Maccabees later reconsecrated the Temple but, successful as the Jews were against Antiochus, internal social damage had been done because the campaign had necessitated fighting on the Sabbath. A core of ultra-strict Jewish devotees known as the Hasidim (Pious Ones) strongly objected to this and, when the triumphant House of Maccabaeus took control and set up their own King and High Priest in Jerusalem, the Hasidim not only voiced their opposition but marched *en masse* out of the city in order to establish their own 'pure' community in the nearby Wilderness of Qumrân. Building work started in around 130 BC.

Horsemen of the Hasmonaean Maccabees, who secured Judaean independence from Syria in 163 BC

Many relics of the time have since been discovered and, during the 1950s, more than a thousand graves were unearthed at Qumrân. A vast monastery complex from the second habitation was also revealed, with meeting rooms, plaster benches, a huge water cistern and a maze of water conduits. In the Scribes' room were inkwells and the remains of the tables on which the Scrolls had been laid out - some more than 17 feet (*c.*5 metres) in length.[19] It was confirmed, by archaeologists and scholars, that the original settlement had been damaged in the earthquake and rebuilt by the incoming Essenes in the later Herodian era. The Essenes were one of three main philosophical Jewish sects (the other two being the Pharisees and the Sadducees).

Many biblical manuscripts have been found at Qumrân, relating to such books as Genesis,

Exodus, Deuteronomy, Isaiah, Job and others. There are, in addition, commentaries on selected texts and various documents of law and record. Among these ancient books are some of the oldest writings ever found - predating anything from which the traditional Bible was translated. Of particular interest are certain biblical commentaries compiled by the Scribes in such a way as to relate the Old Testament texts to the historical events of their own time.[20] Such a correlation is especially manifest in the Scribes' commentary on the Psalms and on such prophetical books as Nahum, Habakkuk and Hosea. The technique applied to link Old Testament writings like these with the New Testament era was based on the use of eschatological knowledge[21] - a form of coded representation that used traditional words and passages to which were attributed special meanings relevant to contemporary understanding. These meanings were designed to be recognized only by those who knew the code.

The Essenes were trained in the use of this allegorical code, which occurs in the Gospel texts in particular relation to those parables heralded by the words 'for those with ears to hear'. When the Scribes referred to the Romans, for example, they wrote of the Kittim - ostensibly a name for Mediterranean coastal people. It was also used to denote the ancient Chaldeans, whom the Old Testament describes as 'that bitter and hasty nation which shall march through the breadth of the land to possess dwelling places that are not theirs' (Habakkuk 1:6). The Essenes resurrected the old word for use in their own time and enlightened readers knew that Kittim always referred to Romans.[22]

In order that the Gospels should be beyond Roman understanding, they were largely constructed with dual layers of meaning - evangelical scripture on the surface and political information beneath - and the carefully directed messages were generally based on the substitution codes laid down by the Scribes. However, a

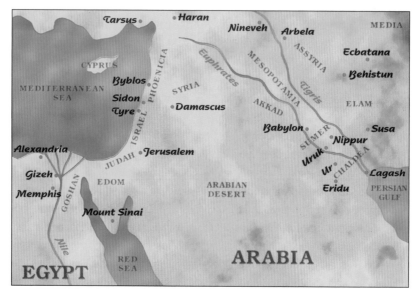

Old Testament Bible Lands

working knowledge of the code was not available until some of the Dead Sea Scrolls were recently published. Only since then has an appreciation of the cryptic technique facilitated a much greater awareness of the political intelligence that was veiled within the Gospel texts. The most extensive work in this field has been conducted by the noted theologian Dr. Barbara Thiering, a lecturer at Sydney University from 1967.

Dr. Thiering explains the code in very straightforward terms. Jesus, for example, was referred to as 'the word of God'. Thus, a superficially routine passage - such as that in 2 Timothy 2:9, 'The word of God is not bound' - would be apprehended at once to concern Jesus, in this case meaning that Jesus was not confined. Similarly, the Roman Emperor was called 'the lion'. Being 'rescued from the lion's mouth', therefore, meant escaping the clutches of the Emperor or his officers.

Study of the Scrolls - particularly the *Pesharim*,[23] *the Manual of Discipline*, the *Community Rule* and the *Angelic Liturgy* - reveals a number of such coded definitions and pseudonyms[24] that were previously misunderstood or considered of no particular importance. For instance, the 'poor' were not poverty-stricken, under-privileged citizens; they were those who had been initiated into the higher echelons of the community and who, on that account, had been obliged to give up their property and worldly possessions. The 'many' was a style used for the head of the celibate community, whereas the 'crowd' was a designation of the regional Tetrarch (Governor) and a 'multitude' was a governing council. Novices within the religious establishment were called 'children'. The doctrinal theme of the community was known as the 'Way' and those who followed the principles of the Way were known as the 'Children of Light'.

The term 'lepers' was often used to denote those who had not been initiated into the higher community, or who had been denounced by it. The 'blind' were those who were not party to the Way and could therefore not see the Light. In these respects, texts mentioning 'healing the blind' or 'healing a leper' refer more specifically to the process of conversion to the Way. Release from excommunication was described as being 'raised from the dead' (a term that is of particular importance and will be returned to later). The definition 'unclean' related mostly to uncircumcised Gentiles, while the description 'sick' denoted those in public or clerical disgrace.

Such information, hidden in the New Testament, was of considerable relevance when written and it remains very important today. Methods of disguising the true meanings included allegory, symbolism, metaphor, simile, sectarian definition and pseudonyms. The meanings were fully apparent, though, to 'those with ears to hear'.

There are, in fact, very similar forms of jargon in modern English. Those of other countries would have difficulty understanding such common English expressions as 'the Speaker addressed the Cabinet', 'the silk prepared his brief', or 'the chair opposed the board'. So too was there an esoteric language of New Testament times - a language that included clouds, sheep, fishes, loaves, ravens, doves and camels. All of these classifications were pertinent, for they were all people - just as are today's screws, fences, sharks, bulls and bears. Currently, we call our top entertainers 'stars', while entertainment investors are called 'angels'. What, then, might an unenlightened reader 2000 years from now make of the statement, 'The angels talked to the stars?'

Additionally, some of the esoteric terms in the New Testament were not merely descriptive of people's social status, but were titles which had special relevance to Old Testament tradition. The doctrine which the community regarded as its guiding message was the 'Light' and this was represented by a high-ranking triarchy (corresponding, respectively, to Priest, King and Prophet) who held the symbolic titles of Power, Kingdom and Glory. In the clerical patriarchy the *Father* was supreme and his two immediate deputies were designated his *Son* and his *Spirit*.[25] (Once again, this is crucial to our story and we shall return to it.)

ARMAGEDDON

Some of the most important non-biblical records of the New Testament era have been preserved in the writings of Flavius Josephus, whose *Antiquities of the Jews* and *Wars of the Jews* were written from a personal standpoint, for he was the military commander in the defense of Galilee during the Jewish Revolt in the first century AD.

Josephus explains that the Essenes were very practiced in the art of healing and received their therapeutic knowledge of roots and stones from the ancients.[26] Indeed, the term 'Essene' may well refer to this expertise, for the Aramaic word *asayya* meant physician and corresponded to the Greek word *essenoi*.

A fundamental belief of the Essenes was that the universe contained the two cardinal spirits of Light and Darkness. Light represented truth and righteousness, whereas Darkness depicted perversion and evil. The balance of one against the other in the cosmos was settled by celestial movement and people were individually apportioned with degrees of each spirit, as defined by their planetary circumstances of birth. The cosmic battle between Light and Darkness was thus perpetuated within humankind and between one person and another: some contained proportionately more Light, others proportionately more Dark.

God was held to be the supreme ruler over the two cardinal spirits, but to find the Way to the Light required following a long and arduous path of conflict. Such a path culminated in a final weighing of one force against the other at a Time of Justification, later called the Day of Judgment. It was thought that, as the time drew near, the forces of Darkness would gather in strength during a Period of Temptation. Those who followed the Way of Light sought to avoid the impending evaluation with the plea, 'Lead us not into Temptation, but deliver us from evil'.

By tradition, the Spirit of Darkness was identified with Belial (Worthless), whose children (Deuteronomy 13:13) worshipped gods other than Jehovah. The Spirit of Light was upheld by the hierarchy and was symbolized by a seven-branched candlestick, the 'Menorah'. In the time of the Davidic kings, the Zadokite priest was considered the foremost proponent of the Light.

Apocalyptic representation of The War in Heaven, by Albrecht Dürer, 1471-1528

But just as the Spirit of Light had its representative on Earth, so too did the Spirit of Darkness. It was an appointment held by the Chief of the Scribes, whose purpose was to provide a formal opposition within the hierarchical structure.[27] A primary responsibility of the designated Prince of Darkness, was to test female initiates within the celibacy, in which capacity he held the Hebrew title of 'Satan' (Accuser). The equivalent title in Greek was *Diabolos* (Aggressor), being the origin of the English word 'Devil'. (The Satan's office was not unlike that of the Devil's Advocate, who probes the background of potential candidates for canonization in the Roman Catholic Church.)

In the book of Revelation (16:16), the great final war between Light and Darkness - between good and evil - is forecast to take place at Armageddon (*Har Megiddo*: the Heights of Megiddo), a historically important Palestinian battlefield where a military fortress guarded the plains of Jezreel, south of the Galilean hills. *The War Scroll* describes in detail the forthcoming struggle between the Children of Light and the Sons of Darkness.[28] The tribes of Israel were to be on one side, with the Kittim (Romans) and various factions on the other. In the context of this climactic war, however, there is no mention of an omnipotent Satan - such mythical imagery played no part in the community's perception of the Final Judgment. The conflict was to be a purely mortal affair between the Light that was Israel and the Darkness of Imperial Rome.

Much later, the fundamental notion behind this ancient concept was purloined and adapted by the emergent Church of Rome. The symbolic battle of Har Megiddo was removed from its specific location and reapplied on a world scale, with Rome (the hitherto 'Darkness') usurping the 'Light' in its own favor. In order that the rule of the Catholic bishops should prevail, it was strategically decreed that the Day of Judgment had

Doctrinal concept of The Last Judgement.
Spanish Church altarpiece, c.1486

not yet come. Those who, thereafter, obeyed the revised principles of the Roman Catholic Church were promised the right of entry to the Kingdom of Heaven, as sanctified by the bishops. The one-time hill-fort of Har Megiddo was thereby invested with supernatural overtones, so that the very word Armageddon took on the hideous ring of apocalyptic terror. It implied the fearsome ending of all things, from which the only sure route to salvation was absolute compliance with the rule of Rome. In this regard, it has proved to be one of the most ingenious political manoeuvres of all time.

3

JESUS, SON OF MAN

THE VIRGIN BIRTH

The Gospels of the New Testament are written in a manner not common to other forms of literature. However, their method of construction was no accident, for they had a common purpose and were not intended to relate history. The aim of the Gospels was to convey an evangelical message (Greek: *eu-aggelos* - 'bringing good news'). The English word 'Gospel' is an Anglo-Saxon translation from the Greek, meaning precisely the same thing.

The original Gospel of Mark was written in Rome in around AD 66. Clement of Alexandria, the second-century churchman, confirmed that it was issued at a time when the Jews of Judaea were in revolt against the Roman occupiers and were being crucified in their thousands. The Gospel writer, therefore, had his own safety to consider and could hardly present a document that was overtly anti-Roman; his mission was to spread the Good News, not to give cause for its condemnation. Mark's Gospel was a message of brotherly support, a promise of independent salvation for those subject to the overwhelming domination of Rome. Such a forecast of deliverance eased the people's minds and took some pressure off the governors whose subjugation was felt throughout the growing Empire.

The Gospel of Mark subsequently became a reference source for those of Matthew and Luke, whose authors severally expanded upon the theme. For this reason, the three are known together as the 'Synoptic Gospels' (Greek: *synoptikos* - '[seeing] with the same eye'), even though they do not concur in many respects.

The Gospel of John differs from the others in content, style and concept, being influenced by the traditions of a particular community sect. It is, nevertheless, far from naive in its account of Jesus's story and, consequently, has its own adherents, who preserve its distinction from the Synoptic Gospels. John also includes countless small details which do not appear elsewhere - a factor that has led many scholars to conclude that it is a more accurate testimony in general terms. The first published Gospel, that of Mark, makes no mention of the Virgin Birth. The Gospels of Matthew

The Adoration of the Magi,
by Domenico Ghirlandaio, 1449-94

and Luke bring it into play with varying degrees of emphasis, but it is totally ignored in John. In the past, as now, clerics, scholars and teachers have thus been faced with the difficulty of analyzing the variant material, as a result of which they have made choices of belief from a set of documents that are very sketchy in places. In consequence, bits and pieces have been extracted from each Gospel, to the extent that a whole new pseudo Gospel has been concocted. Students are simply told that 'the Bible says' this, or 'the Bible says' that. When being taught about the Virgin Birth they are directed to Matthew and Luke. When being taught about other aspects they are directed to the Gospel or Gospels concerned, as if they were all intended to be constituent chapters of the same overall work which, of course, they were not.

Over many centuries, various speculations about biblical content have become interpretations and these have been established by the Church as dogma. The emergent doctrines have been integrated into society as if they were positive facts. Pupils in schools and churches are rarely told that Matthew says Mary was a virgin but that Mark does not; or that Luke mentions the manger in which Jesus was placed whereas the other Gospels do not; or that not one Gospel makes even the vaguest reference to the stable which has become such an integral part of popular tradition. Selective teaching of this kind applies not only to the Bethlehem Nativity, but to any number of incidents in Jesus's recorded life. Instead, Christian children are taught a tale that has been altogether smoothed over; a tale that extracts the most entertaining features from each Gospel and merges them into a single embellished story that was never written by anyone.

The concept of the Virgin Birth of Jesus sits at the very heart of the orthodox Christian tradition. Even so, it is mentioned in only two of the four Gospels and nowhere else in the New Testament. Matthew 1:18-25 reads:

12th-century French stained glass depiction
of Joseph and the Archangel Gabriel

Now the birth of Jesus Christ was on this wise: When as his mother Mary was espoused to Joseph, before they came together, she was found with child of the Holy Ghost.

Then Joseph her husband, being a just man, and not willing to make her a public example, was minded to put her away privily.

But while he thought on these things, behold, the angel of the Lord appeared unto him in a dream, saying, Joseph, thou son of David, fear not to take unto thee Mary thy wife: for that which is conceived in her is of the Holy Ghost. And she shall bring forth a son, and thou shalt call his name Jesus: for he shall save his people from their sins.

Now all this was done, that it might be fulfilled, which was spoken of the Lord by the prophet, saying, Behold, a virgin shall be with child, and shall bring forth a son, and they shall call his name Emmanuel, which being interpreted is, God with us.

The prophet referred to is Isaiah who, in 735 BC, when Jerusalem was under threat from Syria, proclaimed to the troubled King Ahaz, 'Hear ye now, O house of David ... Behold, a virgin shall conceive, and bear a son, and shall call his name Immanuel' (Isaiah 7:13-14).[1] But there is nothing in this to suggest that Isaiah was predicting the birth of Jesus more than 700 years later. Such an anachronistic revelation would actually have been of little use to Ahaz in his hour of need! Like so many instances in the New Testament, this illustrates how events of the Gospels were often interpreted to conform with ambiguous prophecies.

That apart, popular understanding of the Gospel text is based on numerous other misconceptions. The Semitic word translated as 'virgin' was *almah*, which actually meant no more than a 'young woman'.[2] The Hebrew word denoting a physical virgin was *bethulah*. In Latin, the word *virgo* means, quite simply, 'unmarried' and, to imply the modern English connotation of 'virgin', the Latin noun would have to be qualified by the adjective *intacta* (i.e. *virgo intacta*), denoting sexual inexperience.[3]

The physical virginity attributed to Mary becomes even less credible in relation to the dogmatic Catholic assertion that she was a 'virgin forever'.[4] It is no secret that Mary had other offspring, as confirmed in each of the Gospels: 'Is this not the carpenter's son? Is not his mother called Mary and his brethren, James, and Joses, and Simon, and Judas?' (Matthew 13:55). In both Luke 2:7 and Matthew 1:25, Jesus is cited as Mary's 'firstborn son'. The above quotation from Matthew, furthermore, describes Jesus as 'the carpenter's

**Jesus and the Supper at Emmaus,
by Caravaggio, 1601**

son' (that is, the son of Joseph) and Luke 2:27 clearly refers to Joseph and Mary as Jesus's 'parents'. Matthew 13:56 and Mark 6:3 both indicate that Jesus also had sisters.

The portrayal of Jesus as the son of a carpenter is yet another example of how a later language misinterpreted an original meaning. It is not necessarily a deliberate mistranslation, but it does show how some old Hebrew and Aramaic root words, enveloped within the Greek texts, have no direct counterparts in other tongues. The term translated into English as 'carpenter' represents the much wider sense of the ancient Greek *ho tekton* which is a rendition of the Semitic word *naggar*.[5] As pointed out by the Semitic scholar Dr. Geza Vermes, this descriptive word could perhaps be applied to a trade craftsman, but would more likely define a scholar or teacher. It certainly did not identify Jesus and Joseph as woodworkers. More precisely it defined them as men with skills - learned men, who were masters of what they did. Indeed, better translations of the Greek *ho tekton* relate to a Master Craftsman or a Master of the Craft, as might be applicable to modern Freemasonry.

In much the same way, the mention in Luke of the baby Jesus's being placed in a manger has given rise to the whole concept of the Nativity being set in a stable, complete with its familiar cast of attentive animals. But, there is no basis whatever for this image; no stable is mentioned in any original or authorized Gospel. In fact, Matthew 2:11 states quite clearly that the baby Jesus lay within a house: 'And when they were come into the house, they saw the young child with Mary his mother, and fell down, and worshipped him'.[6]

It is also worth noting that the precise words used in Luke 2:7 relate that Jesus was laid in a manger because there was no room *in* the inn',

not '*at* the inn',[7] as is so frequently misquoted. The author and biographer A. N. Wilson specifies, however, that the original Greek (from which the New Testament was translated into English) actually states that there was 'no *topos* in the *kataluma*' - denoting that there was 'no *place* in the *room*'.[8] In reality, it was quite common for mangers (animal feeding boxes) to be taken indoors and used as substitute cradles.

DYNASTIC WEDLOCK

According to Hebrews 7:14, Jesus was of the tribe of Judah. It is evident, therefore, that he was of the family line of King David. The scriptures also say that Jesus was a Nazarene, but this does not mean that he came from the town of Nazareth. Although Luke 2:39 implies that Joseph's family came from Nazareth, the term Nazarene (or Nazarite) was strictly sectarian and had nothing whatever to do with the settlement.

In Acts 24:5, St. Paul is brought on a charge of religious sedition before the Governor of Caesarea: 'For we have found this man a pestilent fellow, and a mover of sedition among all the Jews throughout the world, and a ringleader of the sect of the Nazarenes'. The Arabic term for Christians is *Nasrani* and the Islamic Koran refers to Christians as *Nasara* or *Nazara*. These variants ultimately derive from the Hebrew *Nozrim*, a plural noun stemming from the description *Nazrie ha-Brit* (Keepers of the Covenant), a designation of the Essene community at Qumrân the Dead Sea.[9]

It is actually a point of contention whether the settlement of Nazareth existed at all during Jesus's lifetime, for it does not appear on contemporary maps, neither in any books, documents, chronicles or military records of the period, whether of Roman or local compilation.[10] Even St.

Paul, who relates many of Jesus's activities in his letters, makes no allusion to Nazareth. This being the case, every reference to Nazareth in English translations of the Gospels must be regarded as incorrect - stemming from a misunderstanding of the word 'Nazarene'. As far as has been ascertained, Nazareth (which does not feature in the Hebrew *Talmud*) was of no significance before the Roman destruction of Jerusalem in AD 70, long after the crucifixion of Jesus.

John the Baptist and Jesus's brother James were both Nazarenes, but the older, equivalent sectarian term, Nazarite, can be traced back to the Old Testament figures of Samson and Samuel. Nazarites were ascetic individuals bound by strict vows through predetermined periods, as related in Numbers 6:2-21. In the Gospel era, Nazarites were associated with the Essene community of Qumrân - the environment of Joseph and Mary. The

St. Paul at Ephesus,
by Eustache Le Sueur, c.1648

community observed some highly regulated disciplines in relation to dynastic betrothal and matrimony, so we should refer the question of Mary's said virginity to this specific context.

Both Matthew 1:18 and Luke 2:5 state that Mary was 'espoused' to Joseph and she is thereafter referred to as his 'wife'. As determined in this regard, the word 'espoused' does not mean betrothed or engaged - it refers to contractual wedlock. But, in what circumstance would a married woman also be virginal? To answer this question we must refer to the original Semitic word *almah*, the word that has been translated as virgin' (*virgo*) and incorrectly thought to mean *virgo intacta*.

As we have seen, the real meaning of *almah* was 'young woman' (and it had no sexual connotation). It was quite feasible, therefore, for Mary to be both an *almah* and Joseph's wife. Let us look again at how Matthew describes that, when Joseph learned of Mary's pregnancy, he had to decide whether or not to hide her away. It is of course perfectly normal for a wife to become pregnant, but this was not the case for Mary.

As the wife of a dynastic husband, Mary would have been governed by the regulations applicable to Messianic (anointed) lines such as those of King David and Zadok the Priest. In fact, Mary was serving a statutory probationary period as a married woman of the dynastic hierarchy - a period of espousal during which sexual relations were forbidden - and Joseph would have had just cause for personal embarrassment when Mary was discovered to have conceived. The situation was resolved only when the high-ranking Abiathar priest (the designated Gabriel)[11] granted approval for the confinement.

From the time of King David, the dynasty of Abiathar (2 Samuel 20:25) was established in the hierarchy of senior priests. The line of Zadok was the primary priestly heritage and the line of

The Marriage of Mary and Joseph,
by Ludovicio Carracci, c.1589

Abiathar was second in seniority. In addition to the traditional priestly styles, the Essenes also preserved the names of the Old Testament archangels within their governing structure.[12] Hence, the Zadok priest was also the archangel Michael, while the Abiathar priest (whatever his personal name) was also the angel Gabriel.[13] Being subordinate to the Zadok/Michael (the Lord - 'like unto God'), the Abiathar/Gabriel was the designated 'Angel of the Lord' (the ambassador of the Michael-Zadok). This angelic system is detailed in the Book of 1 Enoch 4:9, whilst the *War Scroll* 9:15-17 identifies the angels' order of priestly ranking during the Gospel era.

In the Luke account, it was through the mediation of the angel Gabriel that Mary's pregnancy was granted approval, being of holy consequence. This is known as the Annunciation, but it was not so much a matter of announcing as one of sanctioning.

Prior to Jesus's birth, the High Zadok (the Michael) was Zacharias. His wife was Mary's cousin Elizabeth[14] and his deputy, the Abiathar (the Gabriel), was Simeon the Essene.[15] It was he who gave the formal consent for Mary's confinement, even though she and Joseph had disobeyed the rules of dynastic wedlock.

It is evident, then, that these dynastic rules were no ordinary matter and were quite unlike the Jewish marital norm.[16] Parameters of operation were explicitly defined, dictating a celibate lifestyle except for the procreation of children and only then at set intervals. Three months after a betrothal ceremony, a First Marriage was formalized to begin the espousal in the month of September. Physical relations were allowed after that, but only in the first half of December. This was to ensure that any resultant Messianic birth occurred in the Atonement month of September. If the bride did not conceive, intimate relations were suspended until the next December, and so on.[17]

**Gabriel's Annunciation to Mary,
by Dante Gabriel Rossetti, c.1849**

Once a probationary wife had conceived, a Second Marriage was performed to legalize the wedlock. However, the bride was still regarded as an *almah* (young woman) until completion of the Second Marriage which, as qualified by Flavius Josephus, was never celebrated until she was three months pregnant.[18] The purpose of this delay was to allow for the possibility of a miscarriage. Second Marriages thus took place in the month of March. The reason that full wedlock was not achieved until pregnancy had been firmly established was to accommodate the dynastic husband's legal change of wife if the first should prove barren.

In the case of Joseph and Mary, it is apparent that the rules of dynastic wedlock were infringed, since Mary gave birth to Jesus at the wrong time of year (Sunday 1 March, 7 BC).[19] Sexual union must therefore have taken place six months before the designated December, in June, 8 BC - at about the time of their initial betrothal - some three months before their First Marriage in the September. And so it was that Mary not only conceived as an *almah*, but also gave birth as an *almah* before her Second Marriage.

Once Mary's unauthorized pregnancy had been confirmed, Joseph would have been granted the choice of not going through with the Second Marriage ceremony. To save embarrassment he could have placed Mary in monastic custody ('put her away privily', as in Matthew 1:19), where the eventual child would be raised by the priests.

But if the child were a boy, he would be Joseph's firstborn descendant in the Davidic succession. It would have made little sense to bring him up as an unidentified orphan, leaving a possible younger brother to become his substitute in the kingly line. Joseph and Mary's unborn child was plainly a significant prospect and demanded special treatment as an exception to the general

rule. The angel Gabriel would, therefore, have advised that, since a sacred legacy was at stake, Joseph should go ahead with the Second Marriage ceremony: 'for that which is conceived in her is of the Holy Ghost' (Matthew 1:20).

Following this dispensation, the normal rules would have been applied once more - the first being that no physical contact was allowed between man and wife until some while after the child had been born: 'Then Joseph being raised from his sleep did as the angel of the Lord had bidden him, and took unto him his wife: And knew her not till she had brought forth her firstborn son: and he called his name Jesus' (Matthew 1:24-25). All that remained was for the Gospel writers to wrap the whole sequence in a blanket of enigma, and this was made possible by the Old Testament prophecy of Isaiah.

DECENT FROM KING DAVID

Strange as it may seem, the Gospel of Mark - from which both Matthew and Luke took their leads - makes no mention of the Nativity. John 7:42 does allude to the birth at Bethlehem, but not as a mysterious event. Neither does John suggest that Mary's conception was virginal. In fact, the Gospel refers only to Jesus's Davidic descent: 'Hath not the scripture said, that Christ cometh of the seed of David, and out of the town of Bethlehem, where David was?' Even the Gospel of Matthew, which implies the notion of Virgin Birth, opens with the statement, 'The book of the generation of Jesus Christ, the son of David, the son of Abraham'.

Paul's Epistle to the Romans 1:3-4 refers to 'Jesus Christ our Lord, which was made of the seed of David according to the flesh; And declared to be the Son of God'. Again, in Mark 10:47 and Matthew

**18th-century carved Spanish altarpiece
denoting the genealogical tree of Jesus**

22:42 Jesus is called the 'Son of David'. In Acts 2:30, Peter, referring to King David, calls Jesus the 'fruit of his loins, according to the flesh'.

All things considered, the divinity of Jesus is figuratively portrayed, whereas his human descent from David ('in accordance with the flesh') is consistently stated as a matter of fact.[20] Indeed, Jesus generally referred to himself as the 'Son of Man' (as for instance in Matthew 16:13). When asked by the High Priest whether he was in truth the Son of God, Jesus replied, 'Thou hast said' - implying that the priest had said it, not he (Matthew 26:63-64). In Luke 22:70, Jesus answered in virtually identical terms: 'Then said they all, Art thou then the Son of God? And he said unto them, Ye say that I am'.

THE MESSIANIC DISPUTE

One of Jesus's foremost problems was that he had been born into an environment of controversy over whether or not he was legitimate. It was for that very reason that Mary and Joseph took him to Simeon the Gabriel for legitimizing under the Law (Luke 2:25-35). Despite this endeavour by his parents, Jesus evoked a mixed response and the Jews were polarized in two opposing camps on the subject of his lawful status in the kingly line. He had been conceived at the wrong time of year and had been born before Joseph and Mary's wedlock was formalized by their Second Marriage. Six years later his brother James was born within all the rules of dynastic wedlock and there was no disputing his legitimacy. Hence, the opposing factions each had a prospective Messiah to support.

The Hellenists (westernized Jews) claimed that Jesus was the rightful Christ (Greek: *Christos* - King), whereas the orthodox Hebrews contended that the kingly entitlement lay with James. The argument persisted for many years but in AD 23 Joseph - the father of both candidates - died and it became imperative to resolve the dispute one way or the other.

Through long prevailing custom, the Davidic kings were allied to the dynastic Zadokite priests and the prevailing Zadok was Jesus's own kinsman, John the Baptist.[21] He had risen to prominence in AD 26 upon the arrival of the Roman governor, Pontius Pilate. John the Baptist was very much of the Hebrew persuasion, but Jesus was a Hellenist. John therefore supported James, even though he acknowledged Jesus as legitimate and baptized him in the Jordan. It was because of the Baptist's attitude that Jesus realized he must make a stand, for if the prospect of a revived Jewish kingdom were to gain momentum he would undoubtedly lose out to his brother James. In view of this, he decided to create his own organized party of supporters: a party that would not follow any conventional social policy. His vision was straightforward, based upon the logic that a split Jewish nation could never defeat the might of Rome. But he perceived too that the Jews could not accomplish their mission if they continued to hold themselves separate from the Gentiles (native non-Jews). Jesus's ambition for the Kingdom of Israel was one of harmonious, integrated society, but he was more than frustrated by the unbending Jews of rigid Hebrew principle.

And so, at length, Jesus stepped into the public domain, resolving to give the people their long-awaited Messiah. After all, he was the firstborn son of his father, no matter what the wrangling priests and politicians had to say on the subject. In a short while he gathered his disciples, appointed his twelve Apostles (delegates) and began his ministry. In this, he sought acceptance in a world where he perceived no selection by class, conviction or fortune - promoting an ideal of princely service that was to carve its mark in time.

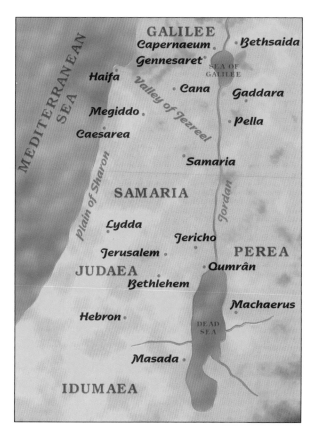

Gospel Locations

THE EARLY MISSION

WHO WERE THE APOSTLES?

For all his apparent humility, there is very little to portray anything faint-hearted or pacifist about Jesus. He knew full well that his task would make him unpopular with the authorities. Not only would the Romans be at his heels, but so too would the Jews' own governing body of legal elders, the powerful Sanhedrin Council. Regardless, Jesus made his entry in due accord, stating at the outset, 'Think not that I am come to send peace on earth: I came not to send peace, but a sword' (Matthew 10:34).

Jesus and the Apostles,
by William Hole, c.1890

Under those circumstances, it seems rather odd that a group of everyday working men would give up their livelihoods for a leader who announced, 'Ye shall be hated of all men for my name's sake' (Matthew 10:22). There was no formal Christianity to preach in those early times and Jesus promised neither earnings nor public status. However, the Gospels appear to indicate that his envoys forsook their various employments and followed blindly into the unknown to become 'fishers of men'. Who, then, were these mysterious Apostles? Can anything of the Qumrân scribal codes be applied to the texts, in order to make their identities and purpose more understandable?

Luke (6:13 and 10:1) tells that Jesus appointed eighty-two followers in all; seventy he sent out to preach and twelve were designated his immediate circle, his Apostles. It is no secret to Bible readers that the Apostles were armed, even though Sunday school tradition would have it otherwise. Indeed, Jesus made sure of their martial ability at the very start of his campaign, saying, 'He that hath no sword, let him sell his garment, and buy one' (Luke 22:36).

All four Gospels agree that Simon was the first recruit; three Gospels also mention his brother Andrew. But there is some disagreement between John and the Synoptic Gospels as to precisely where this recruitment took place. It was either at the Sea of Galilee (the Lake of Gennesaret), where the pair were mending their nets, or at a baptism ritual at Bethabara, beyond Jordan. Moreover, the

**The Sermon on the Mount,
by William Hole, c.1890**

accounts differ again as to who was present at the time. John 1:28-43 states that John the Baptist was there, whereas Mark 1:14-18 claims that it all happened while the Baptist was in prison.

The account in John's Gospel is undoubtedly the more correct, for the first disciples were recruited in March AD 29. In *The Antiquities of the Jews*, Flavius Josephus of Galilee (born AD 37) indicates that Jesus began his ministry in the fifteenth year of the rule of Tiberius Caesar - that is AD 29. John the Baptist was not discredited until a year later in March AD 30 (as confirmed in John 3:24). He was executed by Herod the Great's successor, Herod-Antipas of Galilee, in September AD 31.

Luke 5:11 relates the story of Simon's enlistment as told in the Mark account, but makes no mention of Andrew. Next on the scene are James and John, the sons of Zebedee. Mark and

Luke then declare that Jesus enrolled Levi. In Matthew, however, the next disciple is not called Levi, but Matthew. In John, an early recruit is Philip, who is said to come from Bethsaida, the hometown of Simon and Andrew. Philip, in turn, brought Nathanael of Cana into the fold and, from that point, no more is told of individual appointments.

Instead, it is next explained that Jesus gathered all his disciples together and from them chose his twelve personal delegates. Certain anomalies then become apparent. Levi disappears, as does Nathanael, but Matthew then appears in all listings. The Gospels of Matthew and Mark both name Lebbaeus Thaddaeus as one of the twelve, whereas the other Gospels do not, but Luke and Acts list Judas, the brother of James, in the twelve, whereas he does not appear in this context elsewhere. In Matthew and Mark we are also introduced to Simon the Canaanite, described in Luke and Acts as Simon Zelotes.

Mark narrates how Jesus gave Andrew's brother Simon the name of Peter sometime after their meeting, but Matthew and Luke indicate that he had this other name already. From John we learn that Simon and Andrew were the sons of Jona and that Jesus referred to James and John (the sons of Zebedee) as *Boanerges* or 'Sons of Thunder'. In Mark and Luke, Levi the publican is described as a 'son of Alphaeus', while listed among the final recruits is James, another son of Alphaeus. Thomas, a constant Apostle throughout the Gospels, is referred to in John and Acts as Didymus (the Twin). This leaves only Philip, Bartholomew and Judas Iscariot, each of whom is listed by all the Gospel writers.

It is plain that the Apostles were not a group of sheep-like altruists, who abandoned all to join a charismatic faith healer (even if he was of kingly descent). Jesus's prospects were unknown and, at that stage, he had not gained any divine reputation. It is, therefore, evident that something vital is missing from the Gospels. However, since they were compiled so as not to arouse the suspicions of the Roman overlords, much of their content was phrased in esoteric language for an audience who would understand what was written between the lines.

On many occasions our attention is drawn to specific textual passages by the words, 'He that hath ears to hear, let him hear' (as for instance Mark 4:9). In this regard, we now enter the enlightening world of the New Testament scribal codes - and there is no greater exponent of the ancient translatory art than Dr. Barbara Thiering, whose work is essential reading in this regard. For more than twenty-eight years Dr. Thiering has been concerned with research into the Dead Sea Scrolls and has paved the way to a wealth of new Gospel awareness. We shall now open the door to the Apostles and, in so doing, gain insight into the politically formidable role of Jesus as the Messianic descendant of King David.

JAMES AND JOHN

Jesus referred to James and John (the sons of Zebedee) by the descriptive Greek name of *Boanerges*: the 'Sons of Thunder' (Mark 3:17).This is a positive example of cryptic information aimed at initiates. 'Thunder' and 'Lightning' were the titles of two high-ranking ministers of the Sanctuary. The symbolic titles derived from references to the phenomena at Mount Sinai,[1] described in Exodus 19:16, when thunder and lightning enveloped the mountain and Moses went up from the camp to meet with Jehovah. The Sanctuary was emblematic of the Tabernacle (Exodus 25:8) and the Essene Sanctuary was at the Monastery of Mird, nine miles southeast of Jerusalem - once the site of a Hasmonaean fortress.

The man known to Jesus as 'Thunder' was Jonathan Annas, the son of Ananus, the Sadducee High Priest from AD 6 to 15. Jonathan (which means 'Jehovah gave') was alternatively called Nathanael ('Gift of God'), being essentially the same name. His counterpart and political rival, known as 'Lightning', was Simon Magus (also called Zebedee or Zebadiah: 'Jehovah hath given'), the influential head of the Samaritan Magi. He is better known in the Gospels as Simon the Canaanite or Simon Zelotes.

So, were James and John the sons of Thunder (Jonathan Annas) or the sons of Lightning/Zebedee (Simon Magus)? The answer is that they were both - not by birth, but by distinction. As *Boanerges*, James and John were spiritual sons (deputies) of the Ananus priests; they were also under instruction from Simon, who was destined to hold the highest patriarchal office - that of the community Father.

At once we are presented with a very different picture of the Apostles' social prestige. Even James and John, who are identified as 'fishers', turn out to be prominent in Hellenist society. But why were they depicted (along with Simon-Peter and Andrew) in an environment of fishing boats? This is where the alternative account of John comes into its own, for symbolic fishing was a traditional part of the ritual of baptism.[2]

Gentiles who sought affiliation with the Jewish tribes could take part in the baptism, but could not be baptized in the water. Although they joined the Jewish baptismal candidates in the sea, they were permitted only to receive priestly blessings after they had been hauled aboard ships in large nets. The priests who performed the baptism were called 'fishers'. James and John were both ordained fishers, but Simon-Peter and Andrew were among the lay net-haulers (fishermen). It was in allusion to his own more liberal ministry that Jesus promised them canonical promotion,

saying, 'I will make you to become fishers of men'
(Mark 1:17).

The Apostles were clearly no ragtag band of
righteous devotees, but an influential Council of
Twelve under their supreme leader Jesus the
Christ. Only much later did his royal style, 'Jesus
Christ' (King Jesus), become misconstrued as if it
were a proper name in its own right.[3] It is worth
reminding ourselves here that the Qumrân
Manual of Discipline details the importance of a
Council of Twelve to preserve the faith of the land.

SIMON ZELOTES

Simon Magus (or Zebedee) was head of the West
Manasseh Magi,[4] a priestly caste of Samaritan
philosophers who supported the legitimacy of
Jesus. It was their ambassadors (the Magi, or wise
men) who honored the baby Jesus at Bethlehem.
Simon was a master showman and manuscripts of
his life deal with matters of cosmology, natural
magnetism, levitation and psychokinesis.[5] He was
a confirmed advocate of war with Rome and was
accordingly known as Simon *Kananites* (Greek:
'the fanatic'). This was later mistranslated as Simon
the Canaanite.

As an Apostle of Jesus, Simon was undoubtedly
the most prominent in terms of social status, but
he was also a keen Zealot commander and was
often called Simon *Zelotes* (the Zealot). The Zealots
were militant freedom fighters set on vengeance
against the Romans who had usurped their
heritage and their territory. To the Roman
authorities, however, the Zealots were simply
lestai (bandits).

Already, the Apostles have assumed a more
daunting identity than their familiar image, but
their purpose remains the same: to support and
defend the oppressed of their homeland, being
themselves of the elite class. The majority were

**Familiar conniving image of
Judas Iscariot**

trained priests, therapeutics and teachers; they
would have displayed merciful skills in healing
and been able to expound as orators of great
wisdom and goodwill.

JUDAS ISCARIOT

Another well-born nationalist leader of renown
was Judas, Chief of the Scribes.[6] The Dead Sea
Scrolls were produced under his tutelage and that
of his predecessor, the fierce Judas of Galilee,
founder of the Zealot movement.[7] Apart from his
academic scholarship, Judas the Apostle was the
tribal head of East Manasseh and a warlord of
Qumrân. The Romans had a nickname for him: to
them he was Judas *Sicarius* (a *sica* was a deadly,
curved dagger). The Greek form of the nickname
was *Sikariotes* and its corruption to *Sicariote* was,
in due course, further corrupted to become
'Iscariot'.[8] Although always placed at the end of the
Apostolic lists, Judas Sicariote would have been
second in seniority only to Simon Zelotes.

THADDAEUS, JAMES AND MATTHEW

Lebbaeus Thaddaeus is described as a 'son of Alphaeus' and is also called Judas (Theudas) in two of the Gospels. He was an influential leader of the community and yet another Zealot commander. For more than fifty years, from 9 BC, Thaddaeus was head of the Therapeutate, an ascetic order that had evolved during the Egyptian occupation of Qumrân. Thaddaeus was a confederate of Jesus's father, Joseph, and took part in the people's rising against Pontius Pilate in AD 32.

James, said to be another 'son of Alphaeus', was actually Jonathan Annas, leader of the Thunder Party. The name James is an English variant of the

name Jacob,[9] and the nominal style of Jacob was Jonathan's patriarchal entitlement. Just as the names of the angels and archangels were preserved within the higher priesthood, so too were the Jewish patriarchal names preserved by the community elders. They were led by a triumvirate of appointed officials to whom were applied the titular names Abraham, Isaac and Jacob. In this regard, Jonathan Annas was the Jacob patriarch for a time (the English equivalent being James).

As for Matthew (also called Levi), he too is described as a 'son of Alphaeus'. He was, in fact, Matthew Annas (the brother of Jonathan) - later to succeed as High Priest from AD 42 until deposed by Herod-Agrippa I. Matthew was intimately concerned with the promotion of Jesus's work and actively sponsored the Gospel issued under his name. As Jonathan's successor, he was the chief Levite priest and held the nominal title of 'Levi'. He was also an appointed publican (a Jerusalem tax official), responsible for the collection of public revenues from the Jews who had settled outside their homeland, but were still liable to taxation.[10] Income from Asia Minor was collected by the Levites and deposited at the Treasury in Jerusalem: 'And as Jesus passed forth from thence, he saw a man, named Matthew, sitting at the receipt of custom' (Matthew 9:9). Similarly, in reference to the same event, 'He went forth, and saw a publican, named Levi, sitting at the receipt of custom' (Luke 5:27).

Thaddaeus, James and Matthew (Levi) are all described as 'sons of Alphaeus', but they were not all brothers. As elsewhere, the word 'son' is used to denote a deputy position. The style 'of Alphaeus' did not imply relation to a person or a place, for it meant, quite simply, 'of the Succession'.

Jesus meets with Levi the publican,
by William Hole, c.1890

The body of St. Thomas carried by
Portuguese at Mylapore

PHILIP, BARTHOLOMEW AND THOMAS

As John 1:45-49 indicates, Philip was an associate of Jonathan Annas (alternatively known as Nathanael). An uncircumcised Gentile Proselyte,[11] Philip was head of the Order of Shem.[12] The Coptic Gospel of Philip was written in his name. Bartholomew (also known as John Mark) was Philip's evangelical and political companion. He was chief of the Proselytes and an official of the influential Egyptian Therapeutate (the healing community) at Qumrân.[13]

The Gospels say little about Thomas, but he was among the most influential of Christian evangelists, known to have preached in Syria, Persia and India. He was eventually lanced to death at Mylapore, near Madras. Thomas - originally Crown Prince Philip - was born into the Herod family,[14] but lost his inheritance when his mother, Mariamne II, was divorced by King Herod after she tried to assassinate him. Philip's half-brother, Herod-Antipas, later became Tetrarch of Galilee. In ridicule, the local people likened Prince Philip to Esau - the son of Isaac who lost both his birthright and his father's blessing to his twin brother Jacob (Genesis 25-27) - and they called him *Teoma* (Aramaic for 'twin'): in Greek this name became Thomas and was sometimes translated as Didymus (similarly meaning 'twin').

SIMON-PETER AND ANDREW

We are dealing here with the two Apostles who are often thought to have been the most prominent - yet in this sequence they are placed last. Indeed, the order in which the Apostles have been listed in this section pretty much represents the reverse of that followed in the Gospel lists. This is because such characters as Simon Zelotes, Judas Sicariote and Thaddaeus were far more powerful than their traditional end-of-list positions indicate. But, it was by no accident that the Gospel writers arranged the names as they did for by this means they diverted Roman attention from those Apostles in the very forefront of public life.

Hence, the Apostolic tables usually begin with the least influential members, Simon-Peter and Andrew, who were ordinary village Essenes and held no public office. In the context of their being 'fishermen' and not 'fishers', their role at the baptism ritual was strictly as laymen: they were in charge of the nets, but performed no priestly function (such as the bestowing of blessings) as did the ordained 'fishers' James and John.

For all that, Simon-Peter and Andrew's lack of public station was of great value to Jesus. It made the two brothers more readily available to him than others who had ministerial or legislative work to accomplish. The result was that Simon-Peter became Jesus's right-hand man and he was evidently a fellow of some solidity, being nicknamed Cephas (the Stone). In the Nag Hammadi Gospel of Thomas, Jesus refers to Simon-Peter as his 'guardian' and he was, presumably, Jesus's chief bodyguard. After losing his wife, Simon-Peter became a prominent evangelist and, despite the occasional disagreement with Jesus, was largely responsible for perpetuating the Gospel in Rome. He was, eventually, martyred by crucifixion during Emperor Nero's persecution of the Christians.

PRIESTS AND ANGELS

We have already encountered the fact that the angelic structure was maintained within the priestly hierarchy of the Qumrân community - so that the highest ranking priest was not only the Zadok dynast but was also the archangel Michael. Thus, he was the Michael-Zadok (the Melchizedek). Second in ranking was the Abiathar, who was also the angel Gabriel. It is now worth taking a closer look at the angelic order, for it will shed even

**6th-century mosaic depicting
the fishermen Peter and Andrew**

St. Michael from the 15th-century
Sforza Book of Hours

more light on the Apostles' social status. In this context, various customary practices - both priestly and patriarchal - will become apparent, leading the way, quite naturally, to a whole new understanding of Jesus's miracles.

The first thing to note is that there is nothing spiritual or ethereal about the word 'angel'. In the original Greek, *aggelos* (more usually transliterated as *angelos* - Latin: *angelus*) meant no more than 'messenger'. Modern English derives the word *angel* from this via Church Latin, but the Anglo-Saxon word *engel* came originally from the old French *angele*. An 'angel of the Lord' was, thus, a messenger of the Lord or, more correctly, an ambassador of the Lord. An 'archangel' was a priestly ambassador of the highest rank (the prefix 'arch' meaning 'chief', as in archduke and archbishop).

The Old Testament describes two types of angel, the great majority of whom acted like normal human beings - as for example in Genesis 19:1-3, when two angels visited Lot's house, 'and (he) did bake unleavened bread, and they did eat'. Most Old Testament angels belong to this uncomplicated category, such as the angel who met Abraham's wife Hagar by the water fountain,[15] the angel who stopped Balaam's ass in its tracks,[16] the angel who spoke with Manoah and his wife[17] and the angel who sat under the oak with Gideon.[18]

Another class of angel seems to have been rather more than a messenger, possessing fearsome powers of destruction. This type of avenging angel features in 1 Chronicles 21:14-16: 'And God sent an angel unto Jerusalem to destroy it ... having a sword drawn in his hand stretched out over Jerusalem'. Quite a few angels are described as wielding swords, but they are never said to be divine and there is no hint in the text of the graceful wings that are so often portrayed. The now familiar wings were devised by artists and sculptors to symbolize the angels' spiritual transcendence above the mundane environment.

Notwithstanding the angelic portrayals of the Old Testament, the angels of the New Testament were, without exception, all men and their appointments to angelic office were strictly dynastic. The Book of Enoch (representing the patriarch sixth in line from Adam) was written in the second century BC. It forecast a restoration of the Messianic dynasties and laid down ground-rules for the structure of the priestly hierarchy.[19] Included was the premise that successive dynastic heads should carry the names of the traditional angels and archangels to denote their rank and position.

In the Old Testament days of King David, the senior priests were Zadok, Abiathar and Levi (in that order of precedence). The Essenes of Qumrân duly preserved their priestly heritage using those names as titles: Zadok, Abiathar and Levi, as we have seen. Also, in accordance with the Book of Enoch, the archangelic names were retained, under vow, as badges of priestly rank,[20] with the Zadok dynast being also the Michael; the Abiathar being the Gabriel and the Levi being the Sariel.[21]

We should, therefore, understand that the archangel Michael's battle with the dragon, in Revelation 12:7, corresponds to the conflict between the Zadokite succession and 'the beast of blasphemy' - Imperial Rome. The 'second beast' was that of the rigidly strict regime of the Pharisees, who thwarted the ambitions of the Hellenist Jews by segregating Jews from Gentiles. This was the beast to which was attributed the number 666 (Revelation 13:8) - the numerically evaluated polar opposite to the spiritual energy of water in the solar force.[22]

Outside the dynastic families (the heads of kingly and priestly successions who were expressly required to marry in order to perpetuate their lines), those of the high orders were generally required to remain celibate, as detailed in the *Temple Scroll*. Trainee priests were, therefore, in limited supply and were often raised within a monastic system from the community's illegitimate sons. Jesus might well have become one of those trainee priests, whose mother had been 'put away privily', were it not for the considered intervention of the angel Gabriel.

When procreation was embarked upon, a priestly dynast (such as the Zadok) had, temporarily, to suspend himself from his ordained role and pass his religious duties to another. When physical relations with his wife were completed, he would once more live apart from her and resume his celibate existence.

The Zadok/Michael of the early Gospel era was Zacharias (the husband of Mary's cousin, Elizabeth). His priestly deputy, the Abiathar/Gabriel, was Simeon. The story of Zacharias' procreational leave is very veiled in Luke 1:15-23, but his being rendered 'speechless in the Temple' actually means that he was prevented from speaking in his usual ordained capacity. Being concerned about his advancing age, Zacharias the Zadok transferred his priestly authority to Simeon the Abiathar so that Elizabeth could bear a son. That son was John the Baptist who, in time, succeeded as the Zadokite head.

At the time of Jesus's early ministry, the head of the Levi priests was Jonathan Annas. As chief of the Levite dynasty he held the third archangelic rank of Sariel, in which capacity he was the nominated King's Priest. Along with these three supreme archangels (chief ambassadors), Michael (the Zadok), Gabriel (the Abiathar) and Sariel (the Levi), there were also others with pre-eminent titles. These positions, however, were not dynastic and were denoted by the representative styles, *Father*, *Son* and *Spirit*. The *Father* was the equivalent of the Roman Pope of later times (Pope = Papa = Father) - the Roman style having been purloined directly from the original Jewish source. In essence, the *Son* and *Spirit* were his physical and spiritual deputies. The position of Father was elective and precluded its holder from certain other duties. For example, when Jonathan Annas became the *Father*, his brother Matthew (the Apostle) became his successor as the head of the Levi priests of the Succession. Hence, Matthew then became the 'Levi of Alphaeus'.

The Levi priests (Levites) operated as subordinates of the archangels. At their head, but junior to the Levi dynast, was a Chief Priest (as

**Jesus washing Peter's feet at the Last Supper,
by Ford Maddox Brown, c.1865**

distinct from a High Priest). He was angelically designated Raphael. His senior priests were styled in accordance with the original sons of Levi (as given in Genesis 29:34) and they were called Kohath, Gershon and Merari. The next priest in seniority was Amram (the Old Testament son of Kohath), followed by Aaron, Moses and the priestess, Miriam. They, in turn, were senior to Nadab, Abihu, Eleazar and Ithmar - the representative sons of Aaron.

It is at this stage that the primary aspect of the Grail Code begins to emerge, for the heir to the Davidic kingly succession held no angelic title and was not in priestly service. The King was obliged to serve the people and it was his express duty to champion them against establishment injustice. The very name David means 'beloved' and, as an upholder of this distinction, Jesus would have

made a very fine king. It was this royal concept of humble service that the lay disciples found so hard to comprehend in their Messianic leader. This is well demonstrated in John 13:4-11, when Jesus washed the Apostles' feet. Peter queried the action, saying, 'Thou shalt never wash my feet', but Jesus was insistent, replying with finality, 'I have given you an example, that ye should do as I have done to you'. Such a charitable action is not the mark of a power-seeking dynast, but is emblematic of common fatherhood in the nature of true Grail kingship.

5

THE MESSIAH

WATER AND WINE

Although not considered to be history in the traditional sense, the Gospels relate the story of Jesus by way of a continuous narrative. Sometimes they are in agreement; sometimes they are not but, at all times, their purpose was to convey an imperative social message with Jesus as the focal catalyst. Not all of that message was delivered in an overt fashion, however. Jesus is often said to have spoken in the form of parables, thereby simplifying his message with allegorical discourse. To some, these moralistic tales would appear superficial, but their undertones were frequently political, being based upon actual people and real situations.

The Gospels were constructed in a similar manner and it is important to recognize that many of the stories about Jesus are themselves the equivalent of parables for the benefit of 'those with ears to hear'. This has often led to some perfectly straightforward events being dubbed with supernatural overtones. A good example occurs in John 2:1-10: the story of Jesus substituting the water for wine at the Cana wedding feast. This well-known event was the first of many presumptuous actions by which Jesus made known his intention to circumvent tradition.

Although raised within a strict regime that was influenced by customs and ancient laws, Jesus recognized that Rome could never be defeated while extremes of competitive doctrine existed

Ruler of the Feast and the betrothal at Cana, by Paolo Veronese, c.1560

within the Jewish community itself. There was no such thing as Christianity in those days - the religion of Jesus was Judaism and the Jews all worshipped one God, but even they were split into various factions, each with a different set of community rules. It was generally perceived, however, that Jehovah 'belonged' to the Jews, but Jesus aspired to share Jehovah with the Gentiles in a way that did not require them to take on all the trappings of orthodox Judaism.

Jesus had little patience with the rigorous creeds of Jewish groups like the Pharisees, and he knew the people could not be freed from oppression until they had forsaken their own uncompromising sectarianism. He was also aware that a Messiah had long been anticipated - a savior who was expected to introduce a new era of deliverance. He would, therefore, be revolutionary in outlook and would set himself apart from customary practice. As the heir to the Davidic royal house, Jesus knew that he was qualified to be that Messiah and that, if he should emerge as such, few would be unduly surprised.

What Jesus did not have was any designated social authority - he was neither a reigning King nor a High Priest. However, he paid little heed to such technicalities and proceeded to implement ritualistic changes regardless of his titular deficiency. On his first opportunity at the Cana wedding, he hesitated, claiming, 'Mine hour is not yet come'. But his mother waved aside his lack of entitlement and directed the servants, saying, 'Whatsoever he saith unto you, do it'.

The only account of this appears in John's Gospel, where the incident of the water and wine is described as the first of Jesus's miracles. But, it is not stated that they 'ran out of wine', as is so often misquoted. The text actually says, 'And when they wanted wine, the mother of Jesus saith unto him, They have no wine'. According to the ritual described in the Dead Sea Scrolls, the relevance of this is plain. At the equivalent of Communion, only fully initiated celibates were allowed to partake of wine.[1] All others present were regarded as unsanctified and were restricted to a purifying ritual with water; these included married men, novices, Gentiles and all lay Jews.

The Gospel text continues: 'There were set there six water-pots of stone, after the manner of the purifying of the Jews'. The significance of Jesus's action is that he took it upon himself to break with tradition when he abandoned the water and allowed the 'unclean' guests to take the sacred wine. The ruler of the feast (Greek: *architriclinos*) 'knew not whence it was (but the servants which drew the water knew)'. He did not comment on any marvelous transformation, but simply remarked that he was surprised the good wine had made its appearance at that stage. As Mary declared, when instructing the servants to obey Jesus, the episode 'manifested forth his glory and his disciples believed on him'.

THE KING AND HIS DONKEY

Shortly after Jesus began his mission, John the Baptist was arrested because he had angered Herod-Antipas, the Governor of Galilee. Antipas had married Herodias, the divorced wife of his half-brother, Philip, and the Baptist repeatedly condemned the marriage, declaring that it was sinful. As a result, he was imprisoned for a year and then beheaded. On his ignoble demise, many of his followers turned their allegiance toward Jesus. Some had thought that John was the expected Messiah, but a number of his prophecies had not been fulfilled[2] and so he was discounted in this regard. One of the reasons why John's prophecies proved inaccurate was because of the differences between the commonly used solar and lunar calendars, further complicated by the Julian calendar introduced from Rome.

The Essenes were advocates of the Greek philosopher Pythagoras (*c.* 570-500 BC), who in his great study of arithmetical ratios searched for meaning both in the physical and metaphysical worlds through mathematical proportions. Over the centuries, using his methodology, world events were foretold with surprising accuracy. One particular event so forecast was the beginning of a new World Order, an occurrence that was in many quarters determined to be the advent of the Savior Messiah.

The years (which we now designate BC) were thus already on a predetermined countdown long before Jesus was born. As things turned out, the Messianic forecast was actually seven years astray when applied to Jesus - which explains why he was (as far as we may be concerned) born in the year 7 BC and not in the notional year 0 (754 AUC).[3] But, his brother James was actually born in the right year, as a result of which many considered James to be the legitimate heir. Much later, by way of a new Roman dating system, the notional year 0 was designated AD 1.

In AD 32, Simon Zelotes fell foul of the authorities, having led an unsuccessful revolt against the Governor of Judaea, Pontius Pilate. The reason for the revolt was that Pilate had been using public funds to have his personal water supply improved. A formal complaint was lodged against him in court,[4] whereupon Pilate's soldiers murdered the known complainants. Armed insurrection immediately ensued, led by the prominent Zealots, Simon Zelotes, Judas Sicariote and Thaddaeus. Perhaps inevitably, the revolt failed and Simon was excommunicated by edict of King Herod-Agrippa. Simon's political opponent, Jonathan Annas, was thus enabled to accede to the supreme office of the Father.

Under the Law, excommunication (to be regarded as spiritual execution, or death by decree) took four days for complete implementation. In the meantime, the excommunicatee was dressed in a shroud, shut away and held to be 'sick unto death'. In view of his patriarchal rank up to that point, Simon was incarcerated in the patrimonial burial chamber at Qumrân known as the Bosom of Abraham.[5] His devotional sisters, Martha and Mary, knew that his soul would be forever condemned if he were not reprieved (raised) by the third day and so they sent word to Jesus that Simon was sick (John 11:3).

At first Jesus was powerless to act, for only the Father or the High Priest could perform such a raising (resurrection) and Jesus held no priestly office. It happened, however, that Herod-Agrippa fell into an argument with the Roman governors, losing his jurisdiction to the short-term benefit of his uncle, Herod-Antipas, who had supported the Zealot action against Pilate. Seizing his opportunity, Antipas countermanded the order of excommunication and instructed that Simon should be 'raised from the dead'. Jesus was, therefore, in something of a quandary. He was heir to the kingly line, yet with no formal entitlement, but he wished to come to the aid of his friend and loyal supporter - and so he did. Although the time of spiritual death (the fourth day following excommunication) for Simon had arrived, Jesus decided to presume a priestly function and perform the release. In so doing, he confirmed the spiritually dead Simon's rank as that of Abraham's Steward, Eliezer (corrupted in the Gospels to Lazarus) and summoned him, under that distinguished name, to 'come forth' from Abraham's Bosom.

And so it was that Lazarus was raised from the dead without official sanction from the new Father, neither from the High Priest, nor from the Sanhedrin Council. Jesus had blatantly flouted the rules, but Herod-Antipas then obliged Jonathan Annas to acquiesce in the *fait accompli* and, to the people at large, the unprecedented event was indeed a miracle.

Jesus had effected exactly what he wanted and, with this impressive action behind him, it remained only for him to be formally anointed and to appear before the people as their rightful Messiah in a way that would leave little room for

The Raising of Lazarus,
by Sebastiano del Piombo, 1485-1547

dispute. How the Savior Messiah was to achieve such recognition was long established for it had been prophesied in the Old Testament book of Zechariah (9:9): 'Rejoice greatly, O daughter of Zion; shout O daughter of Jerusalem: behold, thy King cometh unto thee: he is just, and having salvation; lowly, and riding upon an ass'.

The arrangements were made when Jesus and his disciples were in Bethany during the week before Passover, March AD 33. First (as related in Matthew 26:6-7 and Mark 14:3) Jesus was anointed by Mary of Bethany, who poured a precious box of spikenard[6] over his head. A suitable beast of burden was found and, in accordance with Zechariah's prophecy, Jesus rode into Jerusalem.[7]

THE BRIDEGROOM AND THE BRIDE

It has often been said that the New Testament does not state in any forthright manner that Jesus was married. By the same token and more importantly, however, nowhere does it state that he was unmarried. In fact, the Gospels actually contain a number of specific pointers to his married status and it would have been very surprising if he had remained single, for the dynastic regulations were quite clear in this regard.

As we have seen, the rules of dynastic wedlock were no ordinary affair. Explicitly defined parameters dictated a celibate lifestyle except for the procreation of children at regulated intervals. A lengthy period of betrothal was followed by a First Marriage in September, after which physical relationship was allowed in December. If conception took place, a Second Marriage ceremony was then celebrated in March to legalize the wedlock. During that trial period, and until the Second Marriage, whether pregnant or not, the bride was regarded in law as an *almah*

('young woman' or, as so often erroneously cited, 'virgin').

Among the more colorful books of the Old Testament is *The Song of Solomon* - a series of love canticles between a sovereign bride and her bridegroom. The *Song* identifies the potion symbolic of espousal as the aromatic ointment called spikenard.[8] It was the same very expensive spikenard that was used by Mary of Bethany to anoint Jesus's head at the house of Lazarus (Simon Zelotes) and a similar incident (narrated in Luke 7:37-38) had occurred some time earlier, when a woman anointed Jesus's feet with ointment, wiping them afterwards with her hair.

Mary Magdalene anoints the feet of Jesus,
by Tintoretto, 1519-94

John 11:1-2 also mentions this earlier event, then explains how the ritual of anointing Jesus's feet was performed yet again by the same woman at Bethany. When Jesus was seated at the table, Mary took 'a pound of ointment of spikenard, very costly, and anointed the feet of Jesus, and wiped his feet with her hair: and the house was filled with the odour of the ointment' (John 12:3).

In *The Song of Solomon* (1:12) is the bridal refrain, 'While the king sitteth at his table, my spikenard sendeth forth the smell thereof'. Not only did Mary anoint Jesus's head at Simon's house (Matthew 26:6-7 and Mark 14:3), but she also anointed his feet and wiped them afterwards with her hair in March AD 33. Two and a half years earlier, in September AD 30, she had performed this same ritual three months after the Cana wedding feast.

On both occasions the anointing was carried out while Jesus was seated at the table (as defined in *The Song of Solomon*). This was an allusion to the ancient rite by which a royal bride prepared her bridegroom's table. To perform the rite with spikenard was the express privilege of a Messianic bride and was performed solely at the First and Second Marriage ceremonies. Only as the wife of Jesus and as a priestess in her own right could Mary have anointed both his head and his feet with the sacred ointment.

Psalm 23 depicts God, in the male-female imagery of the era, as both the shepherd and the bride. Of the bride, the words say 'Thou preparest a table before me ... thou anointest my head with oil'.[9] According to the sacred marriage rite of ancient Mesopotamia (the land of Noah and Abraham), the Great Goddess, Inanna, took as her bridegroom the shepherd Dumuzi (or Tammuz)[10] and it was from this union that the concept of the Shekinah-and-Jehovah evolved in Canaan through the intermediate deities Asherah and El Elohim.

Pope Gregory I,
590-604

In Egypt, the anointing of the king was the privileged duty of the pharaohs' semi-divine sister-brides. Crocodile fat was the substance used in the anointing because it was associated with sexual prowess - and the word for 'crocodile' in Egyptian was *messeh*, which corresponds to the Hebrew *Messiah*: 'Anointed One'.[11]

Just as the men who were appointed to various patriarchal positions took on names that represented their ancestors - such as Isaac, Jacob and Joseph - so too were the women styled according to their genealogy and rank. Their nominal styles included Rachel, Rebecca and Sarah.[12] Wives of the Zadok and David male lines held the ranks of Elisheba (Elizabeth) and Miriam (Mary) respectively. That is why John the Baptists's mother is called Elizabeth in the Gospels and why Jesus's mother was Mary. It is also why Jesus's own wife would have been a Mary. These women underwent the ceremony of their Second Marriage only once they were three months pregnant, at which time the bride ceased being an *almah* and became a designated *mother*.

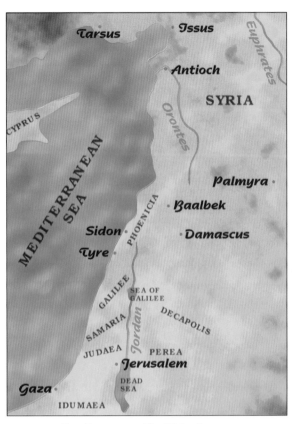

New Testament—The Wider Scene

As we have seen, sexual relations were permitted only in December; husbands and wives lived apart for the rest of the year. At the outset of a period of separation, the wife was classified as a *widow* and was required to weep for her husband. This is described in Luke 7:38, when Mary of Bethany, on the first occasion, is said to have 'stood at his feet behind him weeping, and began to wash his feet with tears'. Once the period of symbolic widowhood had been established, and during these lengthy periods of separation, the wife was given the conventual designation *sister*, just as a modern nun might be. So who exactly was Mary of Bethany - the woman who twice anointed Jesus with spikenard in accordance with Messianic tradition?

To be precise, she is never called 'Mary of Bethany' in the Bible. She and Martha are only ever referred to as 'sisters' at the house of Lazarus of Bethany. Mary's full title was Sister Miriam Magdala or, as she is better known, Mary Magdalene. Gregory I, Bishop of Rome 590-604, and St. Bernard, the Cistercian Abbot of Clairvaux 1090-1153, both confirmed that Mary of Bethany was synonymous with Mary Magdalene.

On the second occasion that Jesus was anointed with spikenard, Judas Sicariote declared his dissatisfaction at the way things were going. He stated his opposition (John 12:4-5) and, thus, paved the way for his betrayal of Jesus. Following the failed revolt by the Zealots against Pilate, Judas had become a fugitive. Jesus was of little political use to him, for he carried no influence with the Sanhedrin Council,[13] so Judas threw in his lot with Jesus's uncontroversial brother James, who was actually a member of that Council. Consequently, Judas not only had no interest in seeing Jesus anointed as a Messiah, but his new allegiance to James caused him to resent it once it had happened. Jesus, nevertheless, was adamant about the significance of his anointing by Mary (Mark 14:9): 'Verily I say unto you, Wheresoever this gospel shall be preached throughout the whole world, this also that she hath done shall be spoken of for a memorial of her'.

Apart from the fact that Jesus was said to love Mary Magdalene, there is not much in the Gospels to indicate their intimate closeness until Mary appears with Jesus's mother and Salome (the consort of Simon Zelotes[14]) at the Crucifixion. Not so, however, in the Nag Hammadi Gospel of Philip, where the relationship between Jesus and Mary is openly discussed:

> And the companion of the Saviour is Mary Magdalene. But Christ loved her more than all the disciples, and used to

kiss her often on the mouth. The rest of the disciples were offended by it and expressed disapproval. They said unto him, Why do you love her more than all of us? The Saviour answered and said to them, Why do I not love you like her? ... Great is the mystery of marriage, for without it the world would not have existed. Now the existence of the world depends on man, and the existence of man on marriage.

There is no talk in John's Gospel of any marriage service at Cana, only of a wedding feast and of the water and wine. The disciples were there, as were various guests including Gentiles and others who were technically 'unclean'. This, then, was not the ceremony of the marriage itself but the sacred meal that preceded the betrothal. The custom was for there to be a formal host (as appears in the account); he would be in full charge as the 'ruler of the feast'. Secondary authority rested only in the bridegroom and his mother - and this is entirely relevant for, when the matter of the communion wine arose, Jesus's mother said to the servants (John 2:5), 'Whatsoever he saith unto you, do it'. No invited guest would have had any such right of command and it is plain, therefore, that Jesus and the bridegroom were one and the same.

This betrothal communion (6 June AD 30) took place three months before Mary first anointed Jesus's feet at Simon's house (3 September AD 30). The rules were strictly defined: only as Jesus's bride would Mary have been permitted to perform this act. With her First Marriage duly completed in the September, she would also have wept for her husband (as in Luke 7:38) before they were parted

for their statutory separation. Prior to this, as a betrothed *almah*, she would have been classified as a *sinner* and ranked as a *crippled woman*.[15] The couple would then not have come together for any physical union until the following December.

SUPPRESSION OF THE MARRIAGE EVIDENCE

One of the reasons why there is no obvious mention of Jesus's marital status in the New Testament is that the evidence was deliberately removed by Church decree. This was revealed as recently as 1958, when a manuscript of the Ecumenical Patriarch of Constantinople was discovered in a monastery at Mar Saba, east of Jerusalem, by Morton Smith, Professor of Ancient History at Columbia University, USA. The extracts quoted below are from his subsequent writings.[16]

Within a book of the works of St. Ignatius of Antioch was a transcription of a letter by Bishop Clement of Alexandria (*c*.AD 150-215). It was addressed to his colleague, Theodore, and included a generally unknown section from the Gospel of Mark. Clement's letter decreed that some of the original content of Mark was to be suppressed because it did not conform with Church requirement. The letter reads:

> For even if they should say something true, one who loves the Truth should not, even so, agree with them. For not all true things are the Truth; nor should that truth which seems true according to human opinions be preferred to the true Truth - that according to the faith.

To them one must never give way; nor, when they put forward their falsifications, should one concede that the secret Gospel is by Mark - but should deny it on oath. For not all true things are to be said to all men.

In the removed section of the Gospel is an account of the raising of Lazarus - but an account that has Lazarus (Simon Zelotes) calling to Jesus from within the tomb even before the stone was rolled back.[17] This makes it quite clear that the man was not dead in the physical sense - which, of course, defeated the Church's insistence that the raising should be accepted as a supernatural miracle. Moreover, the original Gospel of Mark did not include any details of the events of the Resurrection and its aftermath; it ended simply with the women fleeing from an empty sepulchre. The concluding twelve verses of Mark 16, as generally published today, were spuriously attached at a later date.[18]

The relevance of this is that the Lazarus incident was part of that same sequence of events which climaxed when Mary Magdalene anointed Jesus at Bethany. The Synoptic Gospels do not say what happened on Jesus's arrival at Simon's house, for the raising of Lazarus is not included in them, but in John 11:20-29, it is described:

Then Martha, as soon as she heard that Jesus was coming, went and met him: but Mary sat still in the house ...

[Martha] called Mary her sister secretly, saying, The Master is come, and calleth for thee.

As soon as she heard that, she arose quickly and came unto him.

No reason is ventured for Mary's hesitant behaviour although, apart from that, the passage seems straightforward enough. However, the incident is described in much greater detail in the portion of Mark that was officially suppressed. It explains that Mary did come out of the house with Martha on the first occasion, but was then chastised by the disciples and sent back indoors to await her Master's instruction. The fact is that, as Jesus's wife, Mary was bound by a strict code of bridal practice. She was not permitted to leave the house and greet her husband until she had received his express consent to do so.[19] John's account leaves Mary in her rightful place without explanation, but the more detailed Mark text was strategically withheld from publication.

The suppression of the Lazarus story is why the accounts of anointing in the Gospels of Mark and Matthew are located at the house of Simon the leper, instead of at the house of Lazarus as in John. But the description 'Simon the leper' is simply another more guarded way of referring to Simon Zelotes (Lazarus); he was classified as a 'leper' because he was rendered hideously unclean by his excommunication. This, in turn, explains the anomalous account of a leper entertaining prestigious friends at his fine house and the symbolic description of 'leper' was used to veil the truth of the situation. However, the fact was that, with his wife three months into her pregnancy, Jesus was not only a formally anointed Messianic Christ when he rode into Jerusalem on the donkey; he was also a father-to-be.

BETRAYAL

POLITICS AND THE PASSOVER

Jesus rode into Jerusalem in style; coats and palm branches were scattered in this path and there was an amount of cheering, 'Hosanna to the son of David' (Matthew 21:9). It has to be said, however, that this frenetic activity was mainly that of the disciples (as described in Luke 19:36-39). The strewing of the palm fronds was intended to remind the people of the triumphant entry into Jerusalem of Simon Maccabaeus, the deliverer of Palestine from the yoke of Syrian oppression in 142 BC. But Jesus's face was not well known in the city; his familiar territory was Galilee and the land around. Indeed, Matthew 21:10 states:

'And when he was come into Jerusalem, all the city was moved, saying, Who is this?'

A prophecy of John the Baptist[1] had determined that March AD 33 would see the proclamation of the Saviour Messiah and the restoration of the true King. Many things had been carefully prepared for this time - the anointing, the donkey, the palm leaves and so forth - but nothing of consequence happened! According to Mark 11:11, Jesus entered the Temple, 'and when he had looked round and about upon all things, and now eventide was come, he went out unto Bethany'. Luke 19:40 tells that the Pharisees ordered the disciples to be rebuked for creating a disturbance. Matthew 21:12 adds, 'Jesus went into the temple of

Jesus rode into Jerusalem in style,
with palm fronds scattered in this path,
by Hippolyte Flandrin, 1809-64

God, and cast out all them that sold and bought in the temple, and overthrew the tables of the money changers, and the seats of them that sold doves'. He then returned to Bethany.

All things considered, the visit to Jerusalem was an unfortunate non-event. Jesus did not receive the acclaim he expected and he realized that his days were numbered, especially since he was a known associate of the Zealot commanders, Simon Zelotes, Judas Sicariote and Thaddaeus, who had led the revolt against Pilate. The Scribes and priests 'sought how they might take him by craft, and put him to death' (Mark 14:1). His plan to create an idyllic Judaea, free from the Roman oppression, had failed because his dream of unifying the people was not shared by his sectarian countrymen - in particular the stalwart Pharisees and Sadducees.

Also at that time, a serious rift occurred within the Apostolic group. Simon Zelotes had long been at odds with Jonathan Annas (James of Alphaeus) and their political rivalry came to a head. In their respective party roles they were styled Lightning and Thunder, and they were both contenders for the supreme position of Father. Simon was the Father from March AD 31, but lost his supremacy to Jonathan by default through his excommunication. Jonathan had been obliged to endorse the raising of Lazarus (by which Simon was restored to political and social life), but he was in no mood to relinquish the power he had only just gained, especially when Simon had been resurrected against the established rules.

Soon afterwards, it was time for the Jewish celebration of the Passover, when hordes of pilgrims joined the Jerusalem residents for the ritual of the Paschal Lamb in accordance with Exodus 12:3-11. In the course of this, we are told that Jesus and his Apostles made their way to that legendary upper room where they were to eat the

**Judas leaves the Last Supper,
by William Hole, c.1890**

sacred Last Supper. But there are some questionable features about this. How was it that, at such a time when all the temporary accommodation in the city was full to bursting, the Apostles were so easily able to obtain a room of some considerable size for themselves? How also could the fugitive Zealots, Simon, Judas and Thaddaeus, possibly afford to move openly in Jerusalem, while being sought for leading the recent revolt?

The answer to these questions may be found in the Dead Sea Scrolls, wherein it is evident that the Last Supper did not take place in Jerusalem at all, but at Qumrân. Indeed, Josephus explains in *The*

Antiquities of the Jews that the Essenes did not observe the traditional Jewish festivals in Jerusalem[2] and did not, therefore, uphold the ritual of the Paschal Lamb at the Passover.

More than 160 years earlier, when the pious Hasidim vacated Jerusalem for Qumrân in around 130 BC, their new environment became a substitute Holy City. The custom was continued by the later Essenes and, in this context, they often referred to Qumrân as 'Jerusalem' (*Yuru-salem*: City of peace). As evidenced by one of the Dead Sea Scrolls known as the *Community Rule*, the famous Last Supper corresponds, in fact, to the Messianic Banquet (the Lord's Supper). That it occurred at the same time as the Passover celebration in Jerusalem was entirely coincidental, for the Messianic Banquet had a quite different significance. The primary hosts of the Banquet were the High Priest and the Messiah of Israel.[3] The people of the community were represented by appointed officers who together formed the Council of Delegate Apostles. The *Rule* lays down the correct order of precedence for the seating and details the ritual to be observed at the meal. It concludes:

> And when they gather for the community table ... and mix the wine for drinking, let no man stretch forth his hand on the first of the bread or the wine before the Priest, for it is he who will bless the first fruits of the bread and wine ... And afterwards, the Messiah of Israel shall stretch out his hands

upon the bread, and afterwards all the congregation of the community will give blessings, each according to his rank.[4]

When the time came for communion, Judas left the room, ostensibly to offer alms to the poor (John 13:28-30). Actually, he went to make the final arrangements for Jesus's betrayal, while Jesus - who perceived his intention - said, 'That thou doest, do quickly' (John 13:27). There was, however, still time for the Baptist's prophecy concerning the restoration of the true Christ to be fulfilled - but the final deadline was that very night, the vernal equinox of 20 March AD 33.[5] Jesus knew that if this passed with no proclamation being made in his favour, then his ambition was over. From that night there would be no hope of satisfying the Messianic prediction and he would be denounced as a fraud. When Judas left the room, the time was already fast approaching midnight.

Following the banquet, Jesus and the remaining Apostles went to the old monastery at Qumrân, customarily known as the Mount of Olives. There is some disagreement at this point between John's Gospel and the Synoptic Gospels on the precise course of events but, one way or another, Jesus foretold his fate and outlined to his companions what their reactions would be. He declared that even Peter would deny him in the face of the unfulfilled prophecy. While some of Jesus's disciples slept in the monastery garden, Jesus walked among them

Jesus proclaims that he will be denied,
by Edward Deanes (19th century)

The Arrest at Gethsemane,
by Friedrich Overbeck, c.1845

(Matthew 26:36-45), agonizing that his bid to be recognized as the Saviour Messiah might have failed. Midnight passed - then Judas Sicariote arrived with the soldiers.

The ultimate success of Judas's plan relied on retaining favour with the Father, Jonathan Annas. Whether Judas took a calculated gamble or whether he and Jonathan had come to some agreement beforehand is uncertain. But when the moment of seizure came, Jonathan certainly ranged himself alongside Judas. This is not really surprising, for Jonathan's daughter was married to the Pharisee High Priest, Joseph Caiaphas, while both Jonathan and Judas were politically opposed to Jesus's close friend Simon Zelotes. With the Gethsemane arrest duly made, 'the captain and officers of the Jews took Jesus, and bound him, and led him away to Annas first; for he was father-in-law to Caiaphas, which was the high priest that same year' (John 18:12-13).

It seems rather strange that Simon Zelotes, who must surely have been present at these events, is not mentioned in any of the Gospel accounts. Yet in Mark 14:51-52 there is a peculiar veiled reference to a person who might very well have been Simon: 'And there followed him a certain young man, having a linen cloth cast about his naked body ... and he left the linen cloth and fled from them naked'. Fleeing 'naked' could well have been symbolic of Simon's having been 'unfrocked' from his previous high ecclesiastical rank, while for him to be described as a 'young man' indeed relegates him to his newly demoted status as a Community novice following his excommunication.

CRUCIFY HIM!

Jesus's trial was hardly a trial at all and the scenario, as presented in the Gospels, is full of ambiguities. Matthew 26:57-59 describes matters thus: 'They that had laid hold on Jesus led him away to Caiaphas the high priest, where the scribes and the elders were assembled ... Now the chief priests, and elders, and all the council, sought false witness against Jesus'.

Even if all these priests, scribes and elders were somehow conveniently gathered together in the early hours at a moment's notice, the fact remains that it was quite outside the law for the Jewish Council to sit at night. Luke 22:66 indicates that although Jesus was taken firstly to Caiaphas, the Sanhedrin did not meet until it was day. But the meeting would still have been illegal because the Sanhedrin Council was not allowed to sit during the Passover.[6]

The Gospels all state that Peter followed Jesus to the house in which Caiaphas was located, where he denied his master three times as predicted. The house was not in the city of Jerusalem, though; it was the Vestry House at Qumrân.[7] In his capacity as the prevailing High Priest, Caiaphas would necessarily have been at the Messianic Banquet (as laid down in the *Community Rule*) and would, therefore, have been resident in the community along with other officials of the Sanhedrin on the night before the Passover Friday.

All accounts agree that Caiaphas passed Jesus over to the Roman Governor, Pontius Pilate, whose presence facilitated the immediate interrogation. This is confirmed in John 18:28-31, only for a further anomaly to emerge:

> Then led they Jesus from Caiaphas unto the hall of judgement: and it was early; and they themselves went not into the judgement hall, lest they should be defiled; but that they might eat the Passover.
> Pilate then went out unto them, and said, What accusation bring ye against this man?
> They answered and said unto him, If he were not a malefactor, we would not have delivered him up unto thee.
> Then said Pilate unto them, Take ye him, and judge him according to your law. The Jews therefore said unto him, It is not lawful for us to put any man to death ...

In this regard, the truth is that the Sanhedrin was fully empowered not only to condemn criminals but to pass and implement the death sentence if necessary. The Gospels also claim that Pilate offered to reprieve Jesus because 'it was customary for the Governor to release a prisoner

Jesus appears before Pontius Pilate, by William Hole, c.1890

BLOODLINE OF THE HOLY GRAIL

at the feast of the Passover'. Again this is simply not true - there never was such a custom.[8]

Although the Zealots, Simon (Lazarus) and Judas, feature in the events leading to Jesus's arrest, it would appear that Thaddaeus - the third of the key revolutionaries - is not mentioned after the Last Supper. But he does actually come into the story at the trial. Thaddaeus was a deputy of the Succession ('of Alphaeus'), a deputy to the Father and thus a devotional 'son of the Father'. In Hebrew, the expression 'son of the Father' would incorporate the elements *bar* (son) and *abba* (father) - so Thaddaeus might be described as 'Bar-abba' and a man called Barabbas is intimately concerned with the possibility of Jesus's reprieve by Pontius Pilate.

Barabbas is described in Matthew 27:16 as 'a notable prisoner'; in Mark 15:7 as one who had 'committed murder in the insurrection'; in Luke 23:19 as a man who 'for murder had been cast into prison' and in John 18:40 as 'a robber'. The John description is rather too vague, for everyday robbers were not customarily sentenced to crucifixion. However, the English translated word does not truly reflect the original Greek implication, for *léstés* does not mean 'robber' so much as 'outlaw'. Mark's words point far more specifically to the insurgent role of Barabbas in the recent revolt.

What seems to have happened is that when the three prisoners Simon, Thaddaeus and Jesus were brought before Pilate, the cases against Simon and Thaddaeus were clear cut; they were known Zealot leaders and had been condemned men since the uprising. On the other hand, Pilate found it extremely difficult to prove a case against Jesus. Indeed, he was only there because the Jewish contingent had passed him over to Pilate for sentencing with the others. Pilate asked the Jewish hierarchy to provide him, at least, with a pretext - 'What accusation bring ye against this man?' - but received no satisfactory answer. In desperation

'Behold the man'. Pilate offers to spare Jesus.
Antonio Ciseri, 1821-91

Pilate suggested they should take him and 'judge him according to your law', at which the Jews are said to have given the untrue excuse that 'It is not lawful for us to put any man to death'.

So Pilate then turned to Jesus himself. 'Art thou the King of the Jews?' he asked, to which Jesus replied, 'Sayest thou this thing of thyself, or did others tell it thee of me?' Confused by this, Pilate continued, 'Thine own nation and the chief priests have delivered thee unto me: what hast thou done?' The questioning progressed until, eventually, Pilate 'went out again unto the Jews, and saith unto them, I find in him no fault at all' (John 18:38).

At this point, Herod-Antipas of Galilee arrived on the scene (Luke 23:7-12). He was no friend of the Annas priests and it suited his purpose for Jesus to be released in order to provoke his nephew King Herod-Agrippa. Antipas therefore struck a deal with Pilate to secure the release of Jesus. The pact between Judas Sicariote and Jonathan Annas was thus superseded, without involving either of them, by way of an agreement between the Herodian Tetrarch and the Roman Governor. From that moment, Judas lost any chance of a pardon for his Zealot activities and his days were numbered.

In accordance with the new arrangement, Pilate said to the Jewish elders (Luke 23:14-16):

> Ye have brought this man unto me, as one that perverteth the people: and, behold, I, having examined him before you, have found no fault in this man touching those things whereof ye accuse him: No, nor yet Herod: for I sent you to him; and lo, nothing worthy of death is done unto him. I will therefore chastise him, and release him.

Had the members of the Sanhedrin waited until after the Passover, they could have conducted their own trial of Jesus in perfect legality. But they had strategically passed the responsibility over to Pilate because they knew there was no true charge to substantiate. They had certainly not bargained for Pilate's sense of justice, nor for the intervention of Herod-Antipas. But Pilate managed to defeat his own objective. He tried to reconcile his decision to free Jesus with the notion that it might be regarded as a Passover dispensation and, in so doing, he opened the door to a Jewish choice: Jesus or Barabbas? At this, 'they cried out all at once, saying, Away with this man, and release unto us Barabbas' (Luke 23:18).

Pilate pursued his course in favour of Jesus, but the Jews cried 'Crucify him!' Yet again Pilate asked, 'Why, what evil hath he done? I have found no cause of death in him'. But the odds were stacked against him and, giving way to his misguided commitment, Pilate released Barabbas (Thaddaeus). The Roman soldiers placed a crown of thorns on Jesus's head and wrapped a purple robe around him. Pilate then handed him back to the priests, saying, 'Behold, I bring him forth to you, that ye may know that I find no fault in him' (John 19:4).

To Golgotha

At that stage, things were going well for the Jewish elders; their plan had all but succeeded. The ageing Thaddaeus may have been released, but both Simon and Jesus were in custody along with Judas Sicariote. Undoubtedly, the greatest betrayer of all was the prevailing Father, Jonathan Annas, the one-time Apostle known as James of Alphaeus (or Nathanael). The three crosses were duly erected in the 'Place of a Skull' (Golgotha) and were set to bear Jesus and the two Zealot guerrilla leaders, Simon Zelotes and Judas Sicariote.

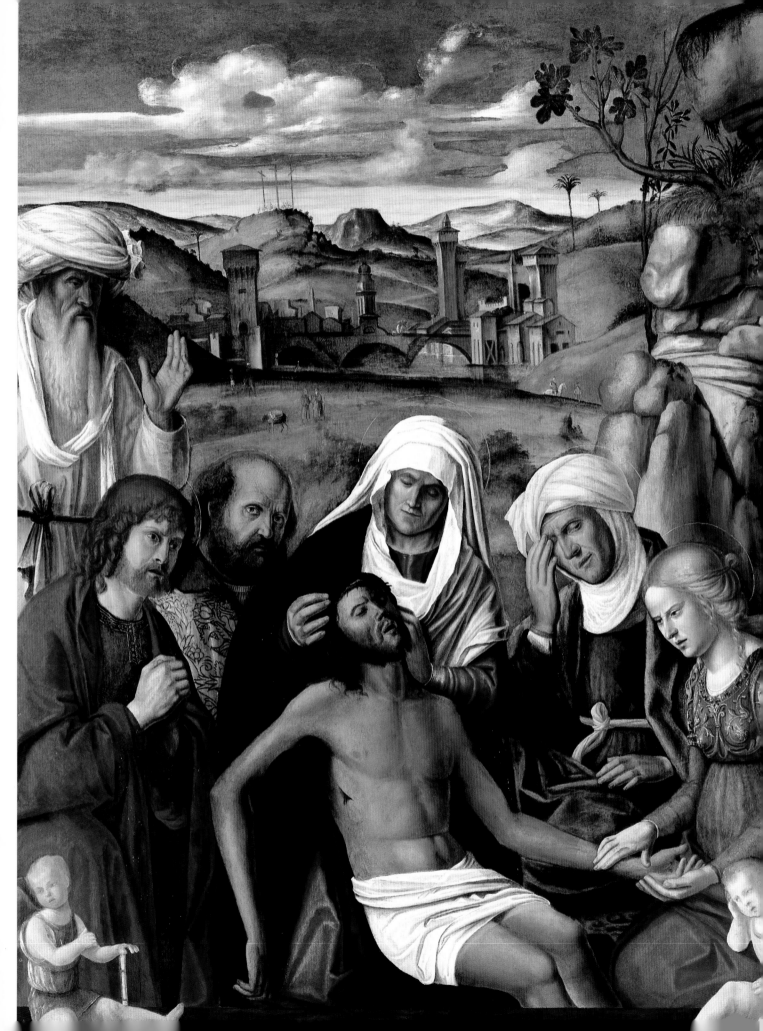